Benjamin Franklin Bush

**A list of the trees, shrubs and vines of Missouri**

Benjamin Franklin Bush

**A list of the trees, shrubs and vines of Missouri**

ISBN/EAN: 9783337225384

Printed in Europe, USA, Canada, Australia, Japan

Cover: Foto ©Andreas Hilbeck / pixelio.de

More available books at **www.hansebooks.com**

# A LIST

# TREES, SHRUBS AND VINES

## OF MISSOURI

---

### B. F. BUSH, Botanist,

*INDEPENDENCE, MO.*

---

*Published in State Horticultural Report, June, 1895.*

JEFFERSON CITY:
TRIBUNE PRINTING COMPANY, STATE PRINTERS AND BINDERS
1895

# THE

# TREES, SHRUBS AND VINES

OF

# MISSOURI

BY

### B. F. BUSH, BOTANIST, INDEPENDENCE, MO.

———

The following list of trees, shrubs and vines of Missouri has been prepared at the request of Mr. L. A. Goodman, Secretary of the Horticultural Society of Missouri, for insertion in their 37th annual report.

The copy has been hastily written for the printer, as the report itself was already in his hands, but it is complete as far as the number of our species is concerned, and no especial effort has been made to learn the complete distribution of each species in the State, and the only reason it is now presented is that it may serve to stimulate our farmers and horticulturists to observe and learn more about the woody plants about them.

As the interest for the study of our plants is awakened in the minds of the people, so in proportion we will know what species we have and their exact distribution throughout the State.

Stretching so far north and south as our State does, we are not surprised that our ligneous flora is so large and greatly diversified, and it is partly on account of its great diversity of species that nothing more is known of it, but more on account of its great diversity of character, which naturally divides the State into four more or less distinct areas. These are as follows: The Northeastern, the Northwestern, the Southeastern and the Southwestern. Each of these areas has a flora that is peculiar to itself—the plants of which are not found in any of the other areas. In the Northeastern we have *Populus tremuloides, Gentiana quinquefolia, Cornus alternifolia, Anemone patens*

H—23

*hirsutissima* and others; in the Northwestern are found *Astragalus loti-florus, Yucca glauca, Meriolix serrulata, Spiesia Lamberti, Penstemon grandiflorus,* and other similar species ; in the Southeastern we find *Leitneria Floridana, ¦Fraxinus Americana profunda, Nyssa uniflora, Trachelospermum difforme* and a hundred others ; in the Southwestern, *Sapindus marginatus, Acacia filiculoides, Toxylon pomiferum, Robinia pseudacacia* and others. The first is clearly the flora of the North-eastern United States. The next is representative of the flora of the plains to the west and northwest. The third is closely related to that of the Southern states; the last partakes of the flora of the South-west.

After a careful and comprehensive study of our woody plants, we find ourselves confronted with a problem that has puzzled many scientific men, and has never been satisfactorily settled; and that is, what are the characteristics of our Flora, and whither is it tending? At the first glance this may not appear very clear to many of my readers, but the full force of the proposition will be seen when I state it thus: what species have we in this State? From whence came they? Are they stationary, or are they moving in any direction? If in any direction, then in what direction? If in some particular direction, then why.? At this point I find myself confronting alternates of opinion which have been advanced by scientific men at various times, and which may continue to be opinions for all time. On the one hand we know this: that the elevation of the State is from the southeast to the north and northwest; all the streams flow south and southeast; a few unimportant only flow west, and none north! The wind is from the north, or some quarter of the north, in the fall and winter when all kinds of seeds and fruits are ripe. Many seed-eating birds and animals migrate regularly from the north to the south in the fall and winter. Does it not seem very natural for plants and seeds to follow the declivity of the land from a high elevation to a lower? How much more easy it is for plants and seeds to drift down the streams toward the south and southeast, than up? In the fall, when the lighter seeds are ripe, whence can they go, except where the north wind blows them? The migratory birds and animals eat many kinds of seeds, and then carry them to the south, where they are deposited, and what choice have they but to grow there?

On the other hand, we know that certain trees follow the streams northwest beyond our limits. All the State is of alluvial character, except a small part near the Ozark region. The prairie region was at one time more extensive than it is now, as it is well-known that the forests are gradually encroaching upon it. The Ozark region only a

short time since was thinly clad with trees, and evidently was com-
pletely bare at one time.

Is it more natural that our trees have come down the rivers from a
prairie region above us, or that they are gradually ascending the streams
and moving to the northwest?  Being of an alluvial formation, must
not the plants that first covered the earth, consequently have been of
a sedgy character, such as grasses and rushes?

As our prairies are becoming smaller and more restricted every
year, are not the trees and shrubs advancing from the streams?  The
Ozark region being thinly clad with trees at one time within the recol-
lection of the oldest settlers, and now being very densely covered
with forests, is it not the more probable that the trees have made their
way up the streams from the southeastern part of the State, and spread
out over these hills?

My opinion is that our ligneous flora is gradually moving up the
streams to the northwest, governed by some influence that I have been
unable to account for at present; but the validity of my position must
be apparent to any one who has given the subject any considerable
study.

Evidently some climatic and other changes are taking place that
are causing the southern and eastern trees to slowly advance to the
northwest, and that our northwestern trees are slowly pushing their
way westward.

The possibilities are very many, and the probabilities many, that
the plants that now grow wild about us unnoticed, except, perhaps, by
a few, will, in time, be found useful and beneficial.  How little we
know of the plums, red-haws, black-haws, raspberries, blackberries,
grapes, crab-apples, service-berries, pawpaw, persimmon and other
wild fruits!  True, there are some who have spent many years of study
upon grapes, plums and the berries, but there are still many promising
wild fruits that may be developed with a little patience and cultivation.

Notes are scattered throughout the list calling attention to those
fruits which are the most promising, and I trust that the farmers and
horticulturists who read this may be stimulated to study and culti-
vate some of the most promising of their locality.

And to the end that a complete history and knowledge of our
native woody plants may be had, it is earnestly requested that teachers,
farmers and horticulturists do all they can to further this by corresponding with the undersigned, and sending twigs, leaves, flowers and
fruit of every woody plant that they desire to learn the name of, and
also of those they already know, that are not credited in this list to the
county in which they live.  By doing this, you will materially aid in the

work of studying the distribution of our woody plants. Twigs, with or without leaves attached, should be 10 to 12 inches long, and may be rolled in paper and transmitted through the mails at the rate of one cent for two ounces. Flowers and leaves may be placed between stiff paste-boards, and tied with a string; and various kinds of fruits, such as acorns, nuts and the like, may be sent in paste-board-boxes. Do not enclose any writing with them, but send a letter accompanying the specimens, stating where they are from, the abundance of the plants, and any other information that may suggest itself to you.

## PINE FAMILY (CONIFERÆ)

1. Pinus echinatus Mill.

*Yellow Pine.* A very valuable tree, found in the State south of a line drawn from the mouth of Meramec river to the southwest corner of the State, and has been found in Barry, Bollinger, Butler, Carter, Christian, Crawford, Dent, Douglas, Howell, Iron, Madison, McDonald, Oregon, Ozark, Perry, Reynolds, Ripley, Shannon, St. Francois, Ste. Genevieve, Taney, Washington and Wayne counties. Probably reaching its highest development in Reynolds, Shannon, Wayne, Carter and Ripley counties. This is *Pinus mitis* Michx.

2. Taxodium distichum (L.) L. C. Rich.

*Bald Cypress.* A large, valuable tree, confined to the lowlands of the southeastern part of the State, and ascending the streams that flow into the southeast. It grows in Bollinger, Butler, Cape Girardeau, Dunklin, Mississippi, New Madrid, Pemiscot, Ripley, Scott and Stoddard counties. Reaches its greatest development in those counties adjacent to the Mississippi river, where there are vast forests of it, and many trees that are 150 feet in height and 30 feet in girth.

3. Juniperus Virginiana L.

*Red Cedar.* A valuable tree, growing naturally in many counties in the State, and probably reaching its greatest development and abundance in Bollinger, Carter, Franklin, Iron, Jefferson, Madison, Shannon, St. Francois, Washington and Wayne counties. Also occurs sparingly and is introduced in Boone, Butler, Callaway, Cape Girardeau, Clark, Cole, Jackson, McDonald, Miller, Newton, Pike, St. Louis and Webster counties. Confined for the greater part to the counties south of the Missouri river.

## LILY FAMILY (LILIACEÆ).

4. Yucca glauca Nutt.

*Soap weed—Bear grass.* Occurs only in the extreme northwestern part of the State, on the high loess mounds in Atchison and Holt counties. The long saponaceous roots are commonly dug by the country people for making soap. This is *Yucca angustifolia* Pursh.

# SMILAX FAMILY (SMILACEÆ).

**5. Smilax bona×Nox L.**

*Greenbrier.* A low, thorny species found in the lowlands of the southern part of the State, in Dunklin, Howell, Jasper, McDonald, Mississippi and Oregon counties.

**6. Smilax glauca Wact.**

*Sawbrier.* A lowland species that is confined to the southeastern part of the State, and found in Bollinger, Butler, Cape Girardeau, Dunklin, New Madrid, Oregon, St. Francois, Stoddard and Wayne counties. In the cotton-raising counties it is a vile pest and is called Sawbrier.

**7. Smilax hispida Muhl.**

*Greenbrier—Catbrier.* Common in many counties in the State, along streams in woods, where it is quite annoying to farmers in clearing new land. It has been found in Atchison, Boone, Butler, Callaway, Cape Girardeau, Clark, Clay, Dunklin, Greene, Jackson, Jasper, Jefferson, McDonald, Newton, Oregon, Pike, Ray, Shannon, St. Francois and Wayne counties.

**8. Smilax pseudo-China L.**

*Sarsaparilla.* Has been reported from Boone, Greene, Pemiscot, Pike and Shannon counties, but it is quite probable that the Boone county and Pike county determinations were based upon some other species of Smilax, as this is a lowland species, and does not occur north of the Missouri river.

**9. Smilax rotundifolia L.**

*Horsebrier—Greenbrier.* A species confined to the southern part of the State, and has been found in Butler, Cape Girardeau, Dunklin, Jasper, McDonald, New Madrid, St. Louis and Wayne counties. Has been reported from Atchison county, by Broadhead, but this was evidently *Smilax hispida*, and also from Pike county by Pech, but it is hardly probable that it gets so far north.

# WALNUT FAMILY (JUGLANDACEÆ).

**10. Juglans cinerea L.**

*White Walnut—Butternut.* Occurs principally in the eastern and southern part of the State, never common at any place. Has been found in Adair, Audrain, Bollinger, Butler, Cape Girardeau, Clark, Dunklin, Greene, Howard, Lafayette, Macon, Madison, Marion, Mississippi, Newton, Pike, Ralls, Saline, Shannon, St. Francois, St. Louis, Stoddard, Sullivan, Washington, Wayne and Wright counties. Not of any economic value, either for its wood or its fruit.

**11. Juglans nigra L.**

*Black Walnut—Walnut.* A very large valuable tree, occurring throughout the State generally, but reaching its greatest development in the southwestern part of the State, where trees are to be found that are three to five feet in diameter. It is known to occur in Adair, Andrew, Atchison, Barry, Benton, Bollinger,

Buchanan, Butler, Cape Girardeau, Carroll, Cedar, Clark, Clay, Dade, Daviess, Dunklin, Greene, Holt, Howard, Jackson, Jefferson, Lawrence, Linn, Madison, McDonald, Mississippi, Newton, Oregon, Platte, Scotland, Shannon, St. Francois, St. Louis, Stoddard, Texas, Vernon, Washington, Wayne and Wright counties.

12. Hicoria alba (L.) Britton.

*Mocker-nut—Black Hickory.* A large, valuable tree with edible nuts. Found in many counties in the State and reported from Adair, Butler, Cape Girardeau, Carter, Clay, Dunklin, Greene, Howell, Jackson, Jasper, Madison, McDonald, Oregon, Shannon, St. Francois, St. Louis, Stoddard, Texas, Wayne and Webster counties. This is *Carya tomentosa* Nutt.

13. Hicoria aquatica ( Michx. f. ) Britton.

*Swamp Hickory.* A southern swamp species that has been reported from Butler county by Letterman, and will probably be found in other parts of the low-lands of the southeastern part of the State. This is *Carya aquatica* Nutt.

14. Hicoria glabra ( Mill.) Britton.

*Pignut Hickory.* A large, valuable tree in the southeastern part of the State, where it abounds, but the nuts are inedible. Has been found in Adair, Atchison, Butler, Daviess, Dunklin, Madison, Pike and St. Louis counties. This and *Hicoria minima* have been confused so much that what was observed at the localities north of the Missouri river may have been the latter. This is *Carya porcina* Nutt.

15. Hicoria laciniosa ( Michx. f.) Sargent.

*Big Shell-bark.* A very large, valuable tree with the largest nuts of our hickories, which are quite excellent eating. Its range is chiefly in the southern part of the State, along streams in lowlands, and has been found in Atchison, Bollinger, Butler, Cape Girardeau, Clark, Dunklin, Jackson, Livingston, Madison, Scotland and St. Louis counties. This is *Carya sulcata* Nutt.

16. Hicoria microcarpa (Nutt.) Britton.

*Small-fruited hickory.* What appears to be this species is found at Allenton, St. Louis county. This is *Carya microcarpa* Nutt.

17. Hicoria minima ( Marsh.) Britton.

*Bitternut.* A valuable tree, bearing inedible nuts, which are commonly called pignut, but this name properly belongs to *Hicoria glabra.* It occurs in many counties and is more widely distributed than pignut. It is found in Atchison, Bollinger, Butler, Clark, Clay, Dunklin, Holt, Jackson, McDonald, Newton, Oregon, Ray, Scotland, Shannon, St. Francois, St. Louis and Wayne counties. This is *Carya amara* Nutt.

18. Hicoria ovata ( Mill.) Britton.

*Shell-bark Hickory—White Hickory.* A very valuable tree, both for lumber and its excellent nuts, which are the principal hickory-nuts of the market. Widely distributed over the whole State, except perhaps the Ozark region, where it does not appear to occur but rarely. An idea may be had of its range in the State when it is known to occur in Adair, Atchison, Bollinger, Butler, Cape Girardeau, Clark, Clay, Daviess, Dunklin, Greene, Holt, Jackson, Jefferson, Madison, McDonald, Mississippi, Pike, Ray, Scotland, Shannon, St. Francois, St. Louis, Stoddard, Texas, Vernon, Washington, Wayne and Wright counties. This is *Carya alba* Nutt.

19. Hicoria Pecan (Marsh.) Britton.

*Pecan.* A very large valuable tree, more esteemed for its excellent fruit than any other tree in the state. The most valuable nuts are those grown in the lowland of the southeastern part of the State. It is found along streams in low land, and grows in Bates, Cape Girardeau, Dunklin, Jackson, Livingston, McDonald, Mississippi, Pike, Platte, St. Louis and Vernon ;counties. This is *Carya olivæformis* Nutt.

## LEITNERIA FAMILY (LEITNERIACEÆ).

20. Leitneria Floridana Chapm.

*Cork-wood-cork-tree.* A southern gulf coast species with remarkably light wood. As shown by me in the fifth annual report of the Missouri Botanical garden, this species, in common with others, works its way up the Mississippi river to the southeastern part of the State, to where evidently an arm of the Gulf of Mexico once extended. The wood is the lightest now known, and is used by fishermen for floats, and other purposes which require a light wood, whence the common names. It has been found in Butler and Dunklin counties.

## WILLOW FAMILY (SALICACEÆ).

21. Populus alba L.

*White poplar.* Commonly planted for ornament, and spreading from the root very much. It has been reported as escaped in Dunklin, Greene, Jackson, Jefferson and Newton counties.

22. Populus balsamifera L.

*Balsam poplar.* Reported from Boone county, but evidently not native there.

23. Populus grandidentata Michx.

*Large-toothed Aspen.* Reported from Boone and Pike counties, but there must be some mistake about this, as I do not think it occurs in the State.

24. Populus heterophylla L.

*Downy Poplar.* This is the congener of the Bald Cypress, as it is found only in the lowlands of the southeastern part of the State. Not of any economic importance, as it does not attain sufficient size to cut into lumber. Is found in Bollinger, Butler, Cape Girardeau, Dunklin, Mississippi, New Madrid, Scott, Stoddard and Wayne counties. It was also reported from Miller by Wirick, but there evidently has been a mistake made in the determination of the tree.

25. Populus monilifera Ait.

*Cottonwood.* A very large valuable tree, reaching its greatest development in the southeast part of the State where trees have been cut that were over seven feet in diameter. This and the Sweet Gum are our two loftiest trees, specimens having been noted that were over 175 feet in height. Occurs abundantly along the Missouri and Mississippi rivers in low bottoms, and common along the smaller streams. Is found in Adair, Andrew, Atchison, Barry, Bollinger, Buchanan, Cape Girardeau, Carroll, Carter, Chariton, Clark, Clay, Daviess, Dunklin, Scott, Jackson, Jasper, Jefferson, Linn, Madison, McDonald, Mississippi, New Madrid, Newton, Platte, Ray, Scotland, Scott, St. Louis, Stoddard, Washington, Wayne and Wright counties.

26.  Populus tremuloides Michx.

*Trembling Aspen.*  A small tree of no economic value, occurring in the north-eastern part of the State.  The peculiar trembling motion of the leaves has given rise to its popular name.  Has been found in Adair, Clark and Sullivan counties; also reported from Franklin county by Swallow, but this must have been an error in determination.

27.  Salix alba L.

*White willow.*  Commonly planted for ornament, and reported as having escaped in the State, by Tracy.

28.  Salix alba vitellina ( L.) Koch.

*Osier willow.*  Like the last, is commonly planted, and has been observed in Jackson, growing along branches.

29.  Salix amygdaloides Anders.

*Almond willow.*  A large tree growing in bottoms along the Missouri and Mississippi rivers.  It has been found in Andrew, Atchison, Cape Girardeau, Clark, Clay, Holt, Jackson, Platte, Scotland and Stoddard counties.

30.  Salix Babylonica L.

*Weeping willow.*  Commonly planted for ornament, and has escaped from culti-vation in Jackson county.

31.  Salix candida Flugge.

*Hoary willow.*  Has been reported from Iron and Pike counties, but I have never seen it in the State.

32.  Salix cordata Muhl.

*Heart-leaved willow.*  A small shrubby tree along branches.  Occurs in Howell, Jackson, Shannon and St. Louis counties.

33.  Salix cordata vestita Anders.

*Diamond willow.*  A larger tree than the last, with very hard wood, which is quite durable, and called Black willow by farmers, a name which properly belongs to *Salix nigra.*  The tree is confined to the rich alluvial bottoms along the Missouri river, and appears quite distinct from the last.  It has been found in Andrew, Atchison, Clay, Holt, Jackson, Platte, Scotland and St. Louis counties.

34.  Salix discolor Muhl.

*Glaucous willow.*  Has been collected in Clark and Pike counties only.

35.  Salix fragilis L.

*Crack willow.*  Reported as collected in Pike county by Pech, but this is probably a mistake.

36.  Salix humilis Marsh.

*Prairie willow.*  A very common bushy willow on the prairies, and becoming a small tree in Jackson county along small streams.  It is found in Atchison, Boone, Carter, Christian, Clark, Greene, Howell, Jackson, Lawrence, McDon-ald, Newton, Shannon, Warren, Wayne, Webster and Wright counties.  The arborescent form was mistaken for *Salix petiolaris* in my Flora of Jackson county, Missouri.

**37. Salix longifolia Muhl.**

*Long-leaved willow.* A very common willow, and one of our most valuable species, inasmuch as it binds the shifting sands on the banks and sand-bars of the Missouri and Mississippi rivers, with its long creeping roots; on which account it is often called Sand-bar willow, and sometimes White willow, a name properly belonging to *Salix alba*. It occurs in Andrew, Atchison, Boone, Buchanan, Clark, Clay, Holt, Jackson, Platte and Putnam counties.

**38. Salix lucida Muhl.**

*Shining willow.* This species is so difficult to distinguish from some forms of *Salix nigra*, that I have some doubt that this species occurs in Jackson county, as reported by me.

**39. Salix nigra Marsh.**

*Black willow.* The largest of our willows, often attaining the height of 125 feet, and having the greatest distribution, but its range appears to extend from the northwestern to the southeastern part of the State; does not appear to be present in the southwestern part of the State, being supplanted by the next tree. It has been observed in Andrew, Atchison, Bollinger, Buchanan, Cape Girardeau, Clay, Dunklin, Holt, Jackson, Jasper, Madison, New Madrid, Pemiscot, Pike, Platte, Ripley, St. Francois, St. Louis, Stoddard and Wayne counties.

**40. Salix nigra Wardi Bebb.**

*Ward's willow.* A species confined to the southwestern part of the State, and did I not have other reasons for thinking this a good species, this difference in range alone would cause me to suspect it. Its present known range is from the mouth of the Kansas river south, and from Little river west, and has been found in Bollinger, Carter, Dade, Greene, Howell, Jackson, Jasper, Lawrence, Madison, McDonald, Newton, Oregon, Shannon, St. Francois, Stoddard, Texas, Wayne and Wright counties.

**41. Salix sericea Marsh.**

*Silky willow.* A species of the low lands adjoining the Mississippi river, and has been found in Cape Girardeau, St. Louis and Washington counties.

**42. Salix tristis Ait.**

*Dwarf gray willow.* A low, bushy species, which has been reported from Greene and Pike counties; but I have never seen it.

## BIRCH FAMILY (BITULACEÆ).

**43. Carpinus Caroliniana Walt.**

*Ironwood — Hornbeam — Blue beech — Water beech.* A small-sized tree, with a smooth trunk and hard, heavy wood, having a range south and east of a line drawn from the northeastern to the southwestern part of the State. It is found in Bollinger, Boone, Butler, Callaway, Cape Girardeau, Clark, Cole, Dunklin, Lincoln, Madison, McDonald, Mississippi, Oregon, Pike, Ralls, Shannon, St. Louis, Stoddard and Wayne counties.

**44. Ostrya Virginiana (Mill.) Willd.**

*Ironwood — Hop hornbeam.* A small-sized tree, with rough bark and very hard, heavy wood, which has a range principally north and west of a line from the north-

H—24

eastern to the southwestern part of the State. Sometimes rarely found in the southeastern part of the State, but very common in the northwestern part. Has been found in Adair, Andrew, Atchison, Butler, Cape Girardeau, Clark, Daviess, Dunklin, Greene, Jackson, Jasper, Madison, McDonald, Oregon, Pike, Randolph, Shannon and St. Louis counties.

### 45.  Corylus Americana Walt.

*Hazelnut* ~ A well-known, widely diffused shrub in the State, commonly found in rich soil in the vicinity of streams. Perhaps occurring in every county in the state, and at present known to grow in Adair, Atchison, Buchanan, Butler, Cape Girardeau, Carter, Clark, Dunklin, Greene, Jackson, Jefferson, Madison, McDonald, Mississippi, Newton, Oregon, Pike, Scotland, Shannon, St. Francois, St. Louis, Sullivan, Texas, Washington, Wayne, Webster and Wright counties.

### 46.  Corylus rostratus Ait.

*Beaked hazelnut.* What appears to be this species has been found in Jackson and Newton counties. It may be distinguished from the last species by the bur which surrounds the nut being of one piece, while the bur of the last is in two pieces.

### 47.  Betula nigra L.

*Red birch—Black birch.* A very common tree south and east of a line drawn from the northeastern to southwestern part of the State. Has a range similar to that of Blue beech and Sassafras, and grows along river courses and around ponds and lakes. It is found in Adair, Audrain, Barton, Bollinger, Butler, Cape Girardeau, Carroll, Carter, Cedar, Chariton, Clark, Dade, Daviess, Dunklin, Henry, Johnson, Linn, Macon, Madison, McDonald, Newton, Pettis, Pike, Randolph, Ripley, Scotland, Shannon, St. Francois, St. Louis, Stoddard, Vernon, Washington and Wayne counties.

### 48.  Betula populifolia Marsh.

*White birch.* A small tree, reported by Tracy as occurring in the State, but has not since been found. Probably the preceding species.

### 49.  Betula pumila L.

*Low birch.* Said to have been found in Washington county by Pech, but I have not seen it.

### 50.  Alnus incana ( L. ) Willd.

*Speckled alder.* Said to have been found in Mississippi county by Galloway, but has not been collected since.

### 51.  Alnus rugosa ( Ehrh.) Koch.

*Smooth alder.* A small shrub found growing along rocky branches, principally in the southern part of the State. Occurs in Bollinger, Butler, Cedar, Cole, Howell, Iron, Lewis, Lincoln, Madison, Marion, Pike, St. Francis, St. Louis, Stoddard, Washington and Wayne counties. This is *Alnus serrulata* Willd.

### OAK FAMILY (Tagaceæ).

### 52.  Fagus atropunicea ( Marsh.) Sudw.

*Beech.* This large valuable tree, whose edible nuts are so well-known, is found only in the southeastern part of the State, generally in rich woods. It is found in

Butler, Cape Girardeau, Dunklin, Madison, Mississippi, Scott, Stoddard and Warren counties. This is *Fagus ferruginea* Ait.

### 53.   Castanea dentata ( Marsh.) Sargent.

*Chestnut.* ' Said by Swallow to grow in New Madrid county, and by Blankin-
ship in Greene county, but probably the next species was what was found. This
is *Castanea sativa Americana* Wats. and Coult.

### 54.   Castanea pumila Mill.

*Chinquapin.* A large tree occurring in the mountaineous regions of the south
part of the State, where it has been found in Barry, Cedar, Jasper, McDonald and
Newton counties. Fruit similar to that of the Chestnut, and often mistaken for it.

### 55.   Quercus alba L.

*White-oak.* One of our most valuab'e, as well as the best known of our oaks.
Reaching its greatest development in the southeastern part of the State, where
there are veritable giants in girth and height. Occurs throughout the State gen-
erally, but principally south of the Missouri river. It is found in Adair, Andrew,
Bollinger, Butler, Cape Girardeau. Carter, Cedar, Clark, Clay, Cole, Dunklin,
Greene, Howard, Howell, Jackson, Jefferson, Lawrence, Livingston, Madison,
McDonald, Mississippi, Newton, Oregon, Platte, Scotland, Shannon, St. Francois,
St. Louis, Stoddard, Sullivan, Texas, Vernon, Washington, Wayne, Webster and
Wright counties.

### 56.   Quercus alba × macrocarpa Eogelm.

A hybrid between the white-oak and bur-oak, of which one tree has been
found in Jackson county.

### 57.   Quercus alba × Muhlenbergii B. F. Bush.

A hybrid between the white-oak and the chinquapin-oak, of which one tree
has been found in Jackson county.

### 58.   Quercus aquatica ( Lam.) Walt.

*Water-oak.* A species of the lowlands of the southeastern part of the State.
A large, valuable tree, bearing a close resemblance to the shingle-oak; is found
in Butler and Dunklin counties, and has been reported from Greene county, but
this must be a mistake in determination.

### 59.   Quercus coccinea Wang.

*Scarlet-oak* What I take to be this species has been found in Jackson and
Shannon counties. There seems to be some doubt about its occurrence in our
borders, although Sargent cites specimens as coming from the northeastern part
of the State. It has also been reported from St. Louis, but that may have been the
Texas red-oak. which is common there, and is commonly mistaken for this species.

### 60.   Quercus digitata ( Marsh.) Sudw.

*Spanish oak.* A large tree of the lowlands of the southeastern part of the
State, of little economic importance. Grows in Butler, Dunklin, New Madrid,
Ripley and Wayne counties. Has been reported from Adair and Livingston
counties by Broadhead, but it is not likely this lowland species should be found
so far north. Also reported from St. Louis county, but this, too, is doubtful, as
the suitable habitat for it is not there. This is *Quercus falcata* Michx.

61.   Quercus imbricaria Michx.

*Shingle oak.*  A very large valuable tree mostly confined to the central part of the State, where it reaches its greatest development. In the early days much used for making shingles, whence the common name. It is found in Adair, Bollinger, Boone, Butler, Cape Girardeau, Carroll, Cass, Clark, Clay, Clinton, Daviess, Dunklin, Greene, Howell, Jackson, Jefferson, Linn, Livingston, Madison, Miller, Oregon, Pike, Ray, Scotland, St. Francois, St. Louis, Stoddard, Sullivan, Washington, Wayne and Webster counties.

62.   Quercus imbricaria×coccinea Engelm.

A hybrid between the Shingle-oak and the Scarlet-oak. This has undoubtedly been found in the State, and I question very much if one of the supposed parents is the Scarlet-oak. Has been found in Butler, Pettis, St. Louis and Washington counties. This is *Quercus Leana* Nutt.

63.   Quercus imbricaria×palustris Engelm.

A hybrid between the Shingle-oak and the Pine-oak ; has been found in St. Louis county.

64.   Quercus imbricaria×rubra B. F. Bush.

A hybrid between the Shingle oak and the Red-oak ; has been found in Jackson county.

65.   Quercus lyrata Walt.

*Overcup-oak.*  A large valuable tree in the lowlands of the southeastern part of the State, where it has been found in Butler, Cape Girardeau, Dunklin, Mississippi, New Madrid, St. Louis and Wayne counties.

66.   Quercus macrocarpa Michx.

*Bur-oak*  One of our largest, and next to the White-oak, the most valuable of our oaks. Distributed over the whole State, but most abundant along the Missouri river in the bottoms.  A pretty fair idea of its range in the State may be had, when we know that it has been found in Adair, Andrew, Atchison, Cape Girardeau, Cedar, Clark, Clay, Clinton, Daviess, Dunklin, Greene, Howard, Jackson, Jasper, Lawrence, Madison, McDonald, Mississippi, New Madrid, Oregon, Pike, Platte, Ray, Scotland, Shannon, St. Louis, Sullivan, Vernon and Wayne counties.

67.   Quercus macrocarpa olivæformis (Michx. f.) A. Gray.

*Dwarf bur-oak.*  A very much dwarfed variety of the last, with smaller oblong acorns and densely pubescent twigs and leaves, which has been found on the sides and tops of the peculiar loess mounds in Atchison county. A small bushy tree 8 to 18 feet in height.

68.   Quercus macrocarpa×Muhlenbergii B. F. Bush.

A hybrid between the Bur-oak and the Chinquapin oak, of which two trees are found in Jackson county.

69.   Quercus macrocarpa×platanoides B. F. Bush.

A hybrid between the Bur-oak and the White-oak, of which quite a grove has been found near Sheffield in Jackson county.

**70. Quercus Michauxii Nutt.**

*Cow-oak.* A lowland species of the southeastern part of the State, where it attains a great height and corresponding girth, and is very valuable for lumber. It occurs in Bollinger, Butler, Cape Girardeau, Dunklin, New Madrid and Stoddard counties.

**71. Quercus minor (Marsh.) Sargent.**

*Post-oak.* A very valuable small-sized tree, reaching its greatest development in and about the Ozark region, where in some places it and the Black-jack oak are the only oaks present. Appears to be absent or very scarce in the northwestern part of the State, as may be seen from the following list of counties, for at present it is known to occur in Adair, Atchison, Barton, Bollinger, Cape Girardeau, Carter, Cedar, Christian, Clark, Dunklin, Greene, Henry, Howard, Howell, Jackson, Jasper, Jefferson, Lawrence, Livingston, Madison, McDonald, Newton, Oregon, Ripley, Shannon, St. Francois, St. Louis, Texas, Wayne, Webster and Wright counties. This is *Quercus stellata* Wang.

**72. Quercus Muhlenbergii Engelm.**

*Chinquapin-oak.* A valuable small-sized tree with very hard wood and edible nuts. Very well known and distributed throughout the State in dry or rocky ground, and is often called Yellow-oak from the yellow inner wood, and Sweet-oak from the edible acorns. It has been found in Andrew, Atchison, Bollinger, Butler, Cape Girardeau, Carroll, Carter, Clark, Clay, Clinton, Dade, Dunklin, Greene, Holt, Howard, Howell, Jackson, Jasper, Jefferson, Livingston, Madison, McDonald, New Madrid, Newton, Oregon, Pike, Platte, Ray, Shannon, St. Francois, St. Louis, Texas, Washington and Wayne counties. Broadhead reported *Quercus Prinus* from Adair county, and Swallow reported it also from Mississippi county, but the Chinquapin-oak was evidently what they had under consideration.

**73. Quercus nigra L.**

*Black jack oak.* A small-sized tree of little value, reaching its greatest development in the Ozark region, where it is in the greatest abundance. Its range is principally, if not entirely, south of the Missouri river, as I have never seen it north of it. It is known to grow in Barton, Bollinger, Carter, Christian, Dunklin, Greene, Howell, Jackson, Jefferson, Lawrence, McDonald, Newton, Oregon, Shannon, St. Francois, St. Louis, Texas, Washington, Webster and Wright counties. Broadhead reported it from Adair and Nodaway counties, but probably erroneously, and Pech is said to have collected it in Pike county.

**74. Quercus palustris Du Roi.**

*Pin-oak.* A common species in low land and swampy places, having a range south and east of a line drawn from the northeastern part of the State to the mouth of the Kansas river; apparently absent from the northwestern part of the State. It is found in Adair, Bollinger, Butler, Cape Girardeau, Clark, Dunklin, Greene, Howard, Howell, Jackson, Mississippi, New Madrid, Pemiscot, Pike, Ray, Shannon, St. Louis, Stoddard, Sullivan and Wayne counties. Commonly called Turkey-oak in the Ozark region, but this name belongs to *Quercus Catesbæi.*

**75. Quercus Phellos L.**

*Willow-oak.* A very valuable tree of the lowlands of the southeastern part of the State, where it is extensively manufactured into lumber and car-timber. It grows in Bollinger, Butler, Dunklin, Madison, Mississippi, New Madrid, Scott and Stoddard counties; was reported from St. Louis by Murtfeldt, but this is probably a mistake.

### 76.   Quercus Phellos×rubra Hollick.

*Bartram's-oak.* A hybrid between some two species of oaks, and not yet definitely settled, but according to the new check-list, between the Willow-oak and the Red-oak. I collected it in Dunklin county, a region in which the Red-oak has been shown not to occur, and Broadhead found it in De Kalb, Shelby and Sullivan counties, and Swallow found it in Cooper and Pettis counties—all localities where the Willow-oak does not grow. It was considered a hybrid between the Willow-oak and the Black-oak by Gray, and to this combination the Willow-oak is an objection, as stated above: Engelmann considered it a hybrid between the Willow-oak and the Scarlet-oak, and as the Scarlet-oak does not extend to the southeastern part of the State, my Dunklin county specimens could not represent this hybrid. This is perhaps the most interesting oak hybrid we have, and has been the subject of much discussion, and is the *Quercus heterophylla* Michx. f.

### 77.   Quercus platanoides (Lam.) Sudw.

*Swamp white-oak.* A large, valuable tree, found mostly north of the Missouri river. It resembles the Bur-oak in appearance of the trunk and leaves, but the acorns are smaller and very long-peduncled; has been found in Adair, Andrew, Cass, Clark, Daviess, Gentry, Jackson, Madison, Saline, Scotland, Sullivan and Worth counties. This is *Quercus bicolor* Willd.

### 78.   Quercus prinoides Willd.

*Prairie-oak—Dwarf Chinquapin-oak.* A low bushy species of the prairie regions of the State, often found loaded with fruit when only a foot or two high. It is often a serious drawback to the farmer in the clearing of land, as it has a habit of stooling out from the main stem for several yards around. Has been found in Atchison, Holt, Howell, Jackson, Shannon, St. Louis and Stone counties.

### 79.   Quercus rubra L.

*Red-oak.* A very large, valuable tree, distributed over the whole of the State, except perhaps the lowlands of the southeastern part, where it is replaced by the Texas red-oak. It reaches its greatest development and abundance along the Missouri river in the central and western part of the State. It occurs in Adair, Andrew, Atchison, Cedar, Clark, Clay, Clinton, Cole, Holt, Howard, Howell, Jackson, McDonald, Newton, Oregon, Pike, Ray, Scotland, Shannon, St. Francois, St. Louis, Wayne, Webster and Wright counties.

### 80.   Quercus rubra runcinata A. D. C.

A variety of the Red-oak, which has been found in Miller and St. Louis counties.

### 81.   Quercus Texana Buckley.

*Texas Red-oak.* A large and valuable oak of Texas, which extends up the Mississippi river as far north as St. Louis, and is the prevailing Red-oak of the lowlands of the southeastern part of the State, where it often has a diameter of five to six feet, and a height of from 100 to 175 feet. So far as I know the range of this species, it occurs in Butler, Dunklin, Mississippi, Ripley and St. Louis counties.

82. **Quercus velutina** Lam.

*Black-oak.* A large and valuable oak, of wide distribution in the State, and reaching its greatest development along the Missouri river in the central and western part of the State. Has been found in Adair, Andrew, Atchison, Buchanan, Butler, Cape Girardeau, Cedar, Clark, Cole, Dunklin, Greene, Holt, Howell, Jackson, Jasper, Lawrence, McDonald, Newton, Oregon, Ripley, Shannon, St. Francois, St. Louis, Sullivan, Texas, Wayne, Webster and Wright counties. This is *Quercus coccinea tinctoria* A. Gray.

## ELM FAMILY (ULMACEÆ).

83. **Ulmus alata** Michx.

*Wahoo elm—Winged elm.* A small tree in most parts of the State where it occurs, reaching its greatest development in the lowlands of the southeastern part of the State, where it often becomes a tree four feet in diameter and 150 feet in height, and where it is known as Red elm, a name properly belonging to *Ulmus pubescens.* Its range is chiefly south of the Missouri river, and it does not appear to occur west of a line drawn from Boonville. At present it is only known to occur in Bollinger, Butler, Callaway, Cape Girardeau, Carter, Cole, Cooper, Dunklin, Howell, Iron, Madison, McDonald, Mississippi, New Madrid, Ripley, Shannon, St. Francois, Stoddard, Warren and Wayne counties.

84. **Ulmus Americana** L.

*White elm.* A large, very valuable tree, both for lumber and ornamenal purposes. Has a wide range throughout the State, and grows in all kinds of soil. Well-grown trees that are found in river bottoms with tall, straight trunks, are sometimes called Hickory elm and Rock elm, a name which properly belongs to *Ulmus racemosa.* It is sometimes called Water elm when found in low grounds, and is most difficult to split, while the form called Rock elm splits remarkably well. It has been found in Adair, Andrew, Atchison, Buchanan, Butler, Cape Girardeau, Carroll, Clark, Clay, Daviess, Dunklin, Greene, Howell, Jackson, Jasper, Lawrence, Madison, McDonald, Newton, Oregon, Pemiscot, Pike, Platte, Ray, Scotland, Shannon, St. Francois, St. Louis, Stoddard, Washington and Wayne counties.

85. **Ulmus pubescens** Walt.

*Red elm—Slippery elm.* A large, valuable tree, found throughout the State in all kinds of soil. Wood reddish, tough and very durable for such purposes as fence posts, rails, fencing. etc. The inner bark very mucilaginous, and much used locally and in medicine. It occurs in Adair, Atchison, Buchanan, Butler, Clark, Dade, Dunklin, Greene, Holt, Howell, Jackson, Madison, McDonald, Mississippi, Newton, Oregon, Ripley, Scotland, Shannon, St. Francois, St. Louis, Stoddard and Wayne counties. This is *Ulmus fulva* Michx.

86. **Ulmus racemosa** Thomas.

*Cork elm, Hickory elm, Rock elm.* A very valuable large elm, found along streams in several counties in the State, and probably more common than is now known, as it closely resembles the White elm, and only a critical examination can distinguish it. It may be recognized by the larger, longer buds, the corky-winged branchlets, and the flowers being racemed instead of in umbels, and produced much later. It is used considerably for making wagon repairs, such as axle-trees, tongues, etc. Has been found thus far in Atchison, Boone, Clark, Dunklin, Jackson and Stoddard counties.

87.  Planera aquatica ( Walt.) J. F. Gmelin.

*Planer-tree.* A small tree much resembling an elm, found in the swamps of the southeastern part of the State. It has a smooth angled trunk and the wood is soft and light. Found only in Dunklin and New Madrid counties.

88.  Celtis Mississippiensis Bosc.

*Yellow hackberry.* A small-sized tree found along the bottoms of the larger streams, and having a smooth trunk with warty pieces scattered over it. The wood is of a beautiful yellow color and is quite soft and very easily split. As I understand the species it is found in Butler, Cape Girardeau, Clay, Dunklin, Jackson, McDonald, Mississippi, New Madrid, Shannon, St. Francois, St. Louis, Stoddard and Wayne counties.

89.  Celtis occidentalis L.

*Hackberry.* A large valuable tree, reaching its greatest development along the Missouri river in the central and western part of the State. The wood is white, very hard and almost uncleavable, and the bark has a peculiar hacked appearance. It occurs in Adair, Atchison, Buchanan, Cape Girardeau, Cedar, Clark, Clay, Daviess, Dunklin, Holt, Howard, Jackson, Madison, McDonald, New Madrid, Oregon, Pike, Ray, Ripley, Scotland, Shannon, St. Francois, St. Louis, Stoddard, Washington and Wayne counties.

90.  Celtis accidentalis pumila (Pursh) A. Gray.

*Low hackberry.* A low shrubby species of hackberry, commonly considered as a variety of the last, but I think it would be better to place it with *Celtis Mississippiensis.* It is found along rocky river banks, mostly in the southern part of the State. It has been found in Howell, McDonald, Newton, Oregon and St. Louis counties. There is a *Celtis* in the southwestern part of the State that may be a new species, but I have been unable to get sufficient material to determine this.

## MULBERRY FAMILY (MORACEÆ).

91.  Morus alba L.

*White mulberry.* Commonly planted for ornament, and formerly for feeding silk-worms, and has become adventive, according to Tracy.

92.  Morus rubra L.

*Mulberry.* A common, well-known, small-sized tree, which is distributed pretty much all over our borders, and which reaches its greatest development in the southeastern part of the State, where trees are frequently met with that are three to four feet in diameter. It occurs in Atchison, Bollinger, Butler, Cape Girardeau, Carter, Clark, Clay, Dade, Daviess, Dunklin, Holt, Jackson, Jefferson, Lawrence, Madison, McDonald, Newton, Oregon, Pike, Platte, Ray, Ripley, Shannon, St. Francois, St. Louis, Stoddard and Wayne counties.

93.  Broussonetia papyrifera L'Her.

*Paper mulberry.* A fast-growing tree, commonly planted for shade in towns in the lowlands of the southeastern part of the State. The soil and climate are so congenial to its nature that it easily escapes from cultivation, and is found growing in many places naturally. I have observed it only in Dunklin county. This tree is not quite hardy enough to stand the severe winter we have in Jackson county, but there is a tree in Robt. Tindall's yard that has been growing there for ten years or more. Sometimes it gets killed down by the frost, but in the spring it will start up afresh, and several times it reached a height of thirty feet or more. For the southern part of the State it will prove a valuable ornamental tree.

94.  Toxylon pomiferum Raf.

*Osage orange.* A shrubby tree, commonly planted for hedges in the prairie regions of the state, and becoming adventive in many counties. Native in Jasper, McDonald and Newton counties, where it becomes a large tree. Has been reported as adventive in Greene, Jackson, Madison, Platte and St. Louis counties. This is *Maclura aurantiaca* Nutt.

### MISTLETOE FAMILY ( LORANTHACEÆ ).

95.  Phoradendron flavescens ( Pursh ) Nutt.

*Mistletoe.* A parasitic shrubby plant found on several species of trees in the southeastern part of the State. Its principal host appears to be the Black gum. I have found it in Butler, Dunklin, New Madrid, Stone and Stoddard counties.

### BIRTHWORT FAMILY ( ARISTOLOCHIACEÆ ).

96.  Aristolochia macrophylla Lam.

*Pipe-vine—Dutchman's Pipe.* Said to have been collected in Mississippi county, but I know nothing of its occurrence in the State. This is *Aristolochia Sipho* L'Her.

97.  Aristolochia tomentosa Sims.

A tall, vigorous climber, with soft spongy stems, and long six-sided pods. Is found in Butler, Dunklin, Greene. McDonald, Shannon, St. Louis, Wayne and Wright counties.

### BUCKWHEAT FAMILY ( POLYGONACEÆ ).

98.  Polygonella Americana ( F. & M.) Small.

A low bushy shrub, with minute leaves, and a profusion of small white flowers; has been collected in Dunklin and Stoddard counties. This is *Polygonella ericoides* Engelm. & Gray.

99.  Brunnichia cirrhosa Banks.

A tall, vigorous climber of the lowlands of the southeastern part of the State. Has been collected in Butler, Dunklin, Mississippi, New Madrid and Stoddard counties.

### MAGNOLIA FAMILY ( MAGNOLIACEÆ ).

100.  Magnolia acuminata L.

*Cucumber-tree.* Has been collected in Stoddard county, by Dodson, but I have not seen it in the State.

101.  Magnolia Virginica L.

*Small magnolia—Sweet bay.* Credited to the State in Torrey & Gray's Flora, but I have not seen it. This is *Magnolia glauca* L.

H—24

102.  Liriodendron Tulipifera L.

*Tulip-tree—White poplar.*  A very valuable large tree of the southern part of the State, generally on the high ridge land.  Specimens 25 feet in circumference and 150 feet in height are not uncommon, and an immense amount of lumber is sawed out of it every year under the name of White poplar.  It grows in Bollinger, Butler, Cape Girardeau, Dunklin, Madison, Mississippi, New Madrid and Stoddard counties.  Wirick reported it from Miller county, but that must have been a mistake.  And Murtfeldt reported it from St. Louis county, but this must evidently have been in cultivation.

## CUSTARD APPLE FAMILY (ANONACEÆ).

103.  Asimina triloba (L.) Dunal.

*Common pawpaw.*  A well-known tree bearing luscious fruit.  This is a very promising fruit, and with a little trouble may be improved very much.  Distributed over the entire State, but appearing rarely in the northeastern part, reaching its greatest development and abundance in the western part of the State along the Missouri river, where specimens have been observed that were 20 inches in diameter.  Its range may be seen from the following list, for it is known to grow in Andrew, Atchison, Bollinger, Butler, Cape Girardeau, Carroll, Clark, Clay, Dade, Dunklin, Greene, Holt, Howard, Jackson, Jefferson, Madison, McDonald, Miller, Mississippi, New Madrid, Newton, Pike, Platte, Ray, Shannon, St. Charles, St. Francois, St. Louis, Stoddard, Washington and Wayne counties.

## CROWFOOT FAMILY (RANUNCULACEÆ).

104.  Clematis Catesbyana Pursh.

A Virgin's-bower that has been lately found in Shannon county by me.

105.  Clematis crispa L.

*Virgin's-bower.*  A southern species which has been found in Dunklin, Mississippi and Scott counties.

106.  Clematis Fremonti S. Wats.

*Virgin's-bower.*  A very local species, and has been found only in Franklin, Jefferson and St. Louis counties.

107.  Clematis Simsii Sweet.

*Leather-flower.*  A trailing or climbing vine, having very peculiar flowers. Found in Bates, Boone, Carroll, Greene, Harrison, Henry, Iron, Jackson, Livingston, Pike, Shannon and St. Louis counties.  This is *Clematis Pitcheri* Torr. & Gray.

108.  Clematis Viorna L.

*Leather-flower.*  Very similar to the last, except that the fruit is very plumose and feathery.  It is found in Butler, Cass, Christian, Greene, Jefferson, McDonald, Oregon, Ozark, Shannon, Stone and Taney counties.

109.  Clematis Virginiana L.

*Common Virgin's-bower.*  A tall-climbing vine with small white flowers, and a dense panicle of white cottony fruits.  Abundant in the swamps of the southeastern part of the State, whence the common name, Nigger-wool and Nigger-wool swamp.  It is known to grow in Atchison, Boone, Butler, Cape Girardeau, Clark, Clay, Cole, Dunklin, Greene, Jackson, McDonald, Mississippi, New Madrid, Pike, Scotland, Shannon, St. Frances, St. Louis and Stoddard counties.

## BARBERRY FAMILY (BERBERIDACEÆ).

**110. Berberis Canadensis Mill.**

*Barberry.* A low, spiny shrub found only on the tops of the high knobs in Shannon county.

**111. Berberis vulgaris L.**

*Common barberry.* Is commonly cultivated, and has been reported by Galloway as having escaped.

## MOONSEED FAMILY (MENISPERMACEÆ).

**112. Menispermum Canadense L.**

*Moonseed.* A woody green climber, with large angled leaves. The long yellow roots are commonly dug for making bitters, and the vine is called Parilla, or Sarsaparilla. Common in rich soil in woods, and has been found in Andrew, Atchison, Butler, Cape Girardeau, Clark, Clay, Dunklin, Greene, Holt, Jackson, Madison, McDonald, Mississippi, Oregon, Platte, Ray, Scotland, Shannon, St. Louis and Wayne counties.

**113. Cebatha Carolina (L.) Britton.**

*Fish-berry.* A tall, climbing woody plant found only south of the Missouri river along river banks. Occurs in Barton, Butler, Cole, Dunklin, Greene, Howell, McDonald, Oregon and Shannon counties. This is *Cocculus Carolinus* D. C.

**114. Calycocarpum Lyoni (Pursh) Nutt.**

*Cup-seed.* A very tall woody climber found along river banks in the State south of the Missouri. Has been found in Dunklin, McDonald, Shannon and St. Louis counties.

## LAUREL FAMILY (LAURACEÆ)..

**115. Sassafras sassafras (L.) Karst.**

*Sassafras.* A well-known tree in many parts of the State, where it is commonly from 10 to 30 feet in height, except in the lowlands of the southeastern part of the State, where it becomes a very large tree, from two to six feet in diameter, and 100 to 150 feet in height. It is mostly confined to the southern part of the State, and does not appear to grow west of a line down from Kirksville to Nevada. It is found in Barry, Bollinger, Butler, Cape Girardeau, Carter, Cedar, Christian, Dunklin, Greene, Howard, Howell, Jasper, Jefferson, Lawrence, Madison, McDonald, Miller, Mississippi, Monroe, New Madrid, Newton, Oregon, Pike, Randolph, Saline, Shannon, St. Francois, St. Louis, Stoddard, Texas, Wayne, Webster and Wright counties. This is *Sassafras officinale* Nees.

**116. Benzoin benzoin (L.) Coulter.**

*Spice-bush.* A well-known shrub found along streams in many parts of the State, mostly south of the Missouri river, and occupying the same range as the Sassafras. Has been found in Barton, Butler, Cape Girardeau, Cedar, Chariton,

Dunklin, Greene, Howard, Jasper, Madison, McDonald, Mississipi, Oregon, Pike, Shannon, Stoddard, Wayne and Wright counties. This is *Lindera Benzoin* Blume.

### 117.   Benzoin melissæfolium (Walt.) Nees.

*Spice-bush.* A species similar to the last, and said to have been collected in Greene county. This is *Lindera melissaefolia* Blume.

## SAXIFRAGE FAMILY (SAXIFRAGACEÆ.)

### 118.   Hydrangea arborescens L.

*Wild hydrangea.* A small shrub found south of the Missouri river in the State. It has been found in Cape Girardeau, Dunklin, Greene, McDonald, Newton, Pike, Shannon, St. Charles, St. Louis, Webster and Wright counties.

### 119.   Hydrangea radiata Walt.

*Wild Hydrangea.* A similar shrub to the last, with densely tomentose leaves ; has been said to have been found in Greene county.

### 120.   Itea Virginica L.

*Itea.* A small shrub found in the swamps of the southeastern part of the State, in Butler, Dunklin and Pike counties.

### 121.   Ribes aureum Pursh.

*Missouri currant.* A yellow-flowered species of the west, and not known certainly to occur in the State, but commonly credited to our territory.

### 122.   Ribes Cynosbati L.

*Prickly gooseberry.* Stems either smooth or prickly, and bearing prickly berries. Has been found in Boone, Clark, Gasconade, Henry, Shannon and St. Louis counties.

### 123.   Ribes floridum L'Her.

*Wild black currant.* This has been found in St. Louis county only.

### 124.   Ribes gracile Michx.

*Missouri gooseberry.* Common in the northern and western part of the State, appearing to be absent from the southeastern part. Found in Adair, Andrew, Atchison, Cape Girardeau, Clark, Clay, Daviess, Holt, Jackson, McDonald, Miller, Pike, Platte, St. Francois, St. Louis and Webster counties. This has commonly been called *Ribes rotundifolium* Michx.

## WITCH-HAZEL FAMILY (HAMAMELIDACEÆ).

### 125.   Hamamelis Virginiana L.

*Witch-hazel.* A curious shrub found along rocky streams in the southeastern part of the State, having the peculiarity of blooming in the fall and winter and ripening its fruit the next year. It has been found in Bollinger, Christian, Iron, Madison, Ozark, Shannon, Stoddard and Wayne counties.

### 126.   Liquidambar Styraciflua L.

*Sweet gum.* A very large tree in the lowlands of the southeastern part of the State, where it sometimes attains a girth of 20 feet and a height of 150 feet. Is cut very extensively into lumber for making tobacco boxes, etc. Grows in Bollinger, Butler, Cape Girardeau, Dunklin, Madison, Mississippi, New Madrid, Scott, Stoddard and Wayne counties. Also has been reported from St. Louis county, but it is not probable that it gets so far north.

## PLANE-TREE FAMILY (PLATANACEÆ).

### 127.  Platanus occidentalis L.

*Sycamore.* A very large, valuable tree found throughout our borders, and reaching its greatest development along the Missouri river in the central and western part of the State. Trees 20 to 25 feet in girth and 100 to 150 feet in height are not rare, and great quantities of it are sawed into lumber for making tobacco boxes, etc. It is found in Andrew, Atchison, Barton, Bates, Bollinger, Buchanan, Butler, Cape Girardeau, Cedar, Clark, Clay, Dade, Daviess, Dunklin, Greene, Holt, Howard, Jackson, Jasper, Jefferson, Lawrence, Macon, Madison, McDonald, Mississippi, New Madrid, Newton, Oregon, Platte, Ray, Scott, Shannon, St. Francois, St. Louis, Stoddard, Texas, Washington, Wayne and Wright counties.

## ROSE FAMILY (ROSACEÆ).

### 128.  Opulaster opulifolius ( L.) Kuntze.

*Nine-bark.* A well-known shrub in many places in the state, and found in Boone, Clark, Cole, Greene, Henry, Howell, Jackson, Jasper, McDonald, Miller Newton, Oregon, Pike, Shannon, St. Charles, St. Louis, Vernon and Wayne counties. This is *Physocarpus opulifolius* Maxim.

### 129.  Spiræa corymbosa Raf.

*Meadow sweet.* Has been found in Putnam county. This is *spiræa betulæfolia corymbosa* Watson.

### 130.  Spiræa salicifolia L.

*Meadow sweet.* Has been found in Boone, Greene and Jackson counties.

### 131.  Spiræa tomentosa L.

*Hard-hack.* Has been found in Boone, Clark, Cooper and Harrison counties.

### 132.  Pyrus angustifolia Ait.

*Narrow-leaved crab-apple.* A species confined to the southwestern part of the State. Has been found in Dunklin, Mississippi, St. Louis and Washington counties. I have never heard of it being grown for its fruit, but it is sometimes planted for ornament.

### 133.  Pyrus coronaria L.

*Crab-apple.* This is the common crab-apple of this State, and is much more common than is now known; but until we can distinguish this with certainty from our other crab-apples, we cannot definitely outline its range. This also is not known to have been grown for its fruit, but is often planted for ornament. At present we know that it grows in Butler, Clark, Daviess, Dunklin, Greene, Jackson, Madison, Miller and Shannon counties.

### 134.  Pyrus Iowensis (Wood) Bailey.

*Iowa crab-apple.*  A very promising crab ; much better than either of the preceding ones, and a distinctively western species. Has been found in Jackson, Shannon, St. Louis and Washington counties. Much more common than these localities indicate, but apparently not distinguished from the last species. In this species the twigs are large and densely tomentose, as are the leaves also, and the fruit is much larger and covered with a gummy secretion. An abundant bearer, this promises very much to become an important addition to our cultivated fruits.

### 135.  Pyrus Malus L.

*Common apple.*  This, or another cultivated species, has been found growing wild in many places in the State, but at present I am unable to say what it is. This genus and Prunus and Vitis are perhaps the most important to horticulturists.

### 136.  Pyrus Soulardi Bailey.

*Soulard crab.*  Of all our crabs this is the most promising, and has already been cultivated for its fruit, and proved to be of great value. Has been found in St. Louis county, and there is a large crab found in Jackson county in the bottoms along the Missouri river that is said to be as large as a Little Romanite, and is much used for making preserves by the country people. I have been unable to secure specimens of this crab here, but it is probable that the Soulard crab extends up the Missouri river bottoms to the western part of the State.

### 137.  Aronia arbutifolia (L.) Ell.

*Choke-berry.*  A low shrub, with small, berry-like fruit, which is very astringent. Has been reported from Atchison county by Broadhead, but probably erroneously. This is *Pyrus arbutifolia* L. f.

### 138.  Amelanchier Botryapium ( L. f.) D. C.

*Service-berry.*  A small tree or bush bearing edible fruit, and which promises to become valuable in the future. It has only been reported from Greene county as yet, but it is very probable that it is common to many other parts of the State. All the Service-berries are susceptible of great improvement by cultivation. This is *Amelanchier Canadensis oblongifolia* T. & G.

### 139.  Amelanchier Canadensis ( L. ) Medic.

*Service-berry.*  A larger tree than the last, and appearing much more common, but probably including two or more species as here given ; and until our forms are carefully studied we cannot with certainty say what species we have, although it is very probable that we have one or two more species than now known. Has been reported from Atchison, Boone, Cape Girardeau, Clark, Greene, Howell, Jackson, Jefferson, Livingston, Madison, McDonald, Miller, Newton, Oregon, Pike, Ripley, Shannon, St. Charles, St. Louis, Wayne, Webster and Wright counties. *Amelanchier Canadensis alnifolia* of my Jackson county list was based on a cultivated tree, and should therefore be excluded from the list.

### 140.  Cratægus apiifolia ( Marsh.) Michx.

*Red-haw.*  A southern species which extends up the Mississippi valley to the southern part of the State ; has been found in Butler county. Bears inedible fruit.

## 141. Cratægus coccinea L.

*Red-haw.* A small tree found mostly in tho southern part of tho State, and bearing inedible fruit. Is found in Cape Girardeau, Jackson, Jasper, McDonald, Shannon and St. Louis counties.

## 142. Cratægus cordata ( Mill.) Ait.

*Red-haw.* A southern species with inedible fruit, which has been found in Boone, Shannon and St. Louis counties.

## 143. Cratægus Crus-galli L.

*Cockspur thorn.* A common thorny bush or low tree, bearing indelible fruit, very common in the prairie regions, and in rocky ground in woods. It has been found in Bollinger, Cape Girardeau, Dunklin, Greene, Juckson, Jasper, Jefferson, McDonald, Miller, Newton, Oregon, Ray, Scotland, Shannon, St. Francois, St. Louis, Texas, Washington and Wayne counties.

## 144. Cratægus Crus-galli ovalifolia Lindl.

*Cockspur thorn.* A variety of the last, which has been found in Barry and Jasper counties.

## 145. Cratægus flava Ait.

*Summer haw.* A small tree, producing edible fruit, which has been found in Boone and Putnam counties.

## 146. Cratægus macracantha Lodd.

*Red-haw* A small tree, but little known, and which has been found only in St. Louis county. This is *Cratægus coccinea macracantha* Dudley.

## 147. Cratægus mollis (T. & G.) Scheele.

*Red-haw.* A large tree found mostly north of the Missouri river, in woods and pastures, and bearing excellent edible fruit. This promises very much to become a valuable addition to our cultivated fruits, as there is a great variety of forms of the fruit, in size, color and quality. Has been found in Andrew, Atchison, Boone, Buchanan, Clark, Greene, Holt, Jackson, Platte, Ray, St. Louis and Webster counties. This is *Cratægus coccinea mollis* T. & G.

## 148. Cratægus Oxyacantha L.

*English Hawthorn.* An introduced species which has escaped in Boone, Montgomery and St. Louis counties.

## 149. Cratægus punctata Jacq.

*Red-haw.* A tree found mostly in the southern part of the State, bearing inedible fruits. Has been found in Barry, Boone, Greene, Jackson, Pike, Shannon and St. Louis counties.

## 150. Cratægus spathulata Michx.

*Red-haw.* A large shrub or small tree of the south, and which has been found in Boone, Miller and St. Charles counties. The fruit is inedible.

## 151. Cratægus tomentosa L.

*Red-ha*-—*Sugar-haw.* A tree common in many places in the State, and very common in and about the Ozark region, where it bears abundantly; the fruit is called sugarhaw, the fruit being very sweet and sugary, and is ripe in October and November. Elsewhere in the State the tree appears to be a shy bearer and the fruit is not quite edible. Has been found in Carter, Clark, Greene, Jackson, McDonald, Miller, Oregon, Phelps, Shannon, St. Charles, St. Louis and Webster counties.

### 152.   Crataegus uniflora Munch.

*Red-haw.* A small shrub one to eight feet in height, bearing inedible fruit. Has been found in Howell, Iron and Shannon counties.   This is *Cratægus parviflora* Ait.

### 153.   Cratægus viridis L.

*Red-haw.* A southern species which comes up the Mississippi valley to the southern part of the State, and up the Neosho river to the southwestern part. Fruit small and inedible. Has been found in Butler, Cape Girardeau, Dunklin, McDonald, Mississippi, St. Louis and Stoddard counties.

### 154.   Rubus Canadensis L.

*Dewberry.* A very promising fruit, of which we already have several valuable varieties in cultivation. We may have several other species when we come to study them more closely. It has been found in Bollinger, Cape Girardeau, Carter, Clark, Clay, Dunklin, Howell, Jackson, Jasper, Livingston, McDonald, Miller, Newton, Oregon, Pike, Shannon, St. Francois, St. Louis and Stoddard counties.

### 155.   Rubus cuneifolius Pursh.

*Sand blackberry.* Has been found in Pike county, but I know nothing of its value as a fruit, never having seen it in the State.

### 156.   Rubus hispidus L.

*Running Swamp blackberry.* What appears to be this species has been in Jackson county. The fruit is not of any value.

### 157.   Rubus occidentalis L.

*Black raspberry.* This is another valuable fruit, and also has produced many cultivated varieties. The wild fruit is quite variable, some being quite large and much earlier than others. Is found in Atchison, Cape Girardeau, Clark, Jackson, Jasper, Livingston, McDonald, Miller, Newton, Pike, Scotland, Shannon, St. Louis and Wayne counties.

### 158.   Rubus trivialis Michx.

*Low bush blackberry.* A southern species which has been found in the State by Swallow. Fruit small and sour, and of little value.

### 159.   Rubus villosus Ait.

*Blackberry.* This is the Blackberry, *par excellence*, and one of which there is much promise to become a valuable species to select natural varieties from. There is a great variation in the size, earliness and flavor of the wild berries, and by careful selection much may be expected from it. It has been found in Adair, Atchison, Bollinger, Butler, Cape Girardeau, Clark, Clay, Daviess, Dunklin, Howell, Jackson, Jasper, Madison, McDonald, Miller, Mississippi, New Madrid, Newton, Oregon, Pike, Ray, Scotland, Shannon, St. Francois, St. Louis, Texas, Wayne, Webster and Wright counties.

**160. Rosa Arkansana Porter.**

*Prairie-rose.* A very strong-growing, profusely flowering Rose of the prairie regions of the western part of the State. Has been found in Andrew, Atchison, Cass, Holt, Jackson and Madison counties. The last locality may perhaps represent some other species.

**161. Rosa blanda Ait.**

*Low Wild-rose.* A low species found in rocky woods and along rocky banks. May be more common here than is now known. It has been found in Greene county only.

**162. Rosa Carolina L.**

*Swamp-rose.* A large robust species of the lowlands of the southeastern part of the State, often found growing on old logs which are floating in the swamps. Has been found in Bollinger, Boone, Butler, Cape Girardeau, Dunklin, Madison, Miller, New Madrid, Scott, St. Louis and Stoddard counties.

**163. Rosa humilis Marsh.**

*Wild-rose.* The most common species in the State, usually found growing in dry soil. It has been found in Cass, Clark, Holt, Jackson, Jefferson, Madison, Pike and St. Louis counties.

**164. Rosa rubiginosa L.**

*Sweet brier.* Commonly cultivated, and has been found growing spontaneously in Boone, St. Francois and Washington counties.

**165. Rosa setigera Michx.**

*Climbing-rose.* A very common, strong-growing Rose, found throughout the State, and the only Climbing species in America. Many varieties of this are in cultivation, and it well deserves a place among our ornamental plants. It is known to grow in Andrew, Atchison, Barton, Buchanan, Butler, Cape Girardeau, Cass, Clay, Dunklin, Greene, Holt, Jackson, Jasper, Lawrence, Madison, McDonald, Miller, Newton, Pike, Platte, Ray, Shannon, St. Francois, Texas and Webster counties.

**166. Rosa Woodsii Lindl.**

*Low Wild-rose.* A low species found in the southern part of the State in rocky ground. Occurs in Howell, Jackson, Madison, Oregon, Shannon and St. Louis counties.

**167. Prunus Americana Marsh.**

*Wild Yellow or Red plum.* A species occurring in the eastern and southern part of the State. There are many varieties in cultivation, and this is a very promising species to select natural varieties from, for it is immensely variable. It has been found in Adair, Barry, Butler, Dunklin, Franklin, Greene, Howell, McDonald, Mississippi, Montgomery, Newton, Oregon, Pike, Shannon, St. Clair, St. Francois, St. Louis, Wayne and Webster counties.

**168. Prunus Americana mollis T. & Gr.**

*Wild plum.* Perhaps better than the last for fruit, for it appears hardier, and a more prolific bearer. Several good varieties of it are in cultivation already, and it will pay to look after this tree. It has been found in Jackson county only as yet, but it is probable that it is very common in the northern part of the State.

### 169.　Prunus angustifolia Marsh.

*Chickasaw plum.* A southern species, not very hardy at the north, and which has given us several very good varieties in cultivation. It is found in Bates, Cass, Newton, Saline and St. Charles counties. This is *Prunus Chicasa* Michx.

### 170.　Prunus hortulana Bailey.

*Wild Goose plum.* The most promising and the most valuable of all our wild plums, and the original of most of our best cultivated varieties. A distinctively Mississippi valley species, and doubtless the best species we have to select natural varieties from. Is found in Atchison, Cape Girardeau, Cass, Clark, Clay, Jackson, Jasper, Newton, St. Francois and St. Louis counties.

### 171.　Prunus hortulana Mineri Bailey.

*Miner plum.* A variety of the last which has been found in Pike county. This is also an interesting tree, and doubtless will prove to be of great value in cultivation.

### 172.　Prunus Pennsylvanica L. f.

*Wild Red cherry.* Has been cultivated some for its fruit, but does not prove to be very promising. It is found in Adair, Pike and St. Louis counties.

### 173.　Prunus pumila L.

*Dwarf cherry.* Credited to the State in Torrey & Gray's Flora, but I have not seen it.

### 174.　Prunus serotina Ehrh.

*Wild Black cherry.* Not of much account for its fruit, but frequently found in cultivation for ornament. Distributed pretty much all over the State, and found in Atchison, Barry, Barton, Bollinger, Buchanan, Butler, Carroll, Clark, Clay, Dade, Daviess, Dunklin, Greene, Howell, Jackson, Jasper, Jefferson, Lawrence, Linn, Livingston, Madison, McDonald, Miller, Newton, Oregon, Platte, Ray, Scotland, Scott, Shannon, St. Francois, St. Louis, Stoddard, Wayne and Washington counties.

### 175.　Prunus Virginiana L.

*Choke cherry.* A shrub or small tree in the northern part of the State; of little value for the fruit. Has been found in Adair, Andrew, Atchison, Buchanan, Caldwell, Clark, Clinton, Daviess, Holt, Knox, Lewis, Linn, Livingston and Saline counties.

## PULSE FAMILY (LEGUMINOSÆ).

### 176.　Cercis Canadensis L.

*Red-bud.* A small-sized tree, very pretty in cultivation, and found growing throughout the State in woods. Is found in Adair, Andrew, Atchison, Bollinger, Butler, Cape Girardeau, Carter, Cass, Clark, Clay, Cole, Dade, Daviess, Dunklin, Holt, Howard, Jackson, Jasper, Jefferson, Livingston, Madison, McDonald, Miller, Mississippi, Newton, Oregon, Pike, Platte, Ray, Shannon, St. Francois, St. Louis, Stoddard, Wayne and Wright counties.

**177. Gleditschia aquatica Marsh.**

*Water locust.* A southern species, found in the lowlands of the southeastern part of the State. Grows in Cape Girardeau, Dunklin, Howell, Jefferson, Mississippi, New Madrid, St. Charles, St. Louis and Wayne counties.

**178. Gleditschia triacanthos L.**

*H-ney locust.* A large tree found throughout the State in woods. Is found in Adair, Andrew, Atchison, Barry, Bates, Bollinger, Buchanan, Butler, Cape Girardeau, Carroll, Cedar, Clark, Clay, Dade, Davies, Dunklin, Greene, Holt, Howard, Howell, Jackson, Jasper, Jefferson, Lawrence, Livingston, Madison, McDonald, Miller, Mississippi, New Madrid, Newton, Oregon, Pike, Platte, Ray, Ripley, Scotland, Shannon, St. Charles, St. Francois, St. Louis, Stoddard, Texas, Washington, Wayne and Wright counties.

**179. Gymnocladus dioicus (L.) Koch.**

*Coffee-tree.* A tall tree of some little value, but not very common at any place in the State, and is found in Andrew, Atchison, Buchanan, Cedar, Clark, Clay, Holt, Jackson, Jefferson, Livingston, Madison, McDonald, Miller, Pike, Platte, Ray, Scott, St. Francois, St. Louis and Wayne counties. This is *Gymnocladus Canadensis* Lam.

**180. Amorpha canescens Pursh.**

*Lead-plant.* A small shrub found in many places, mostly in the prairie regions of the western part of the State, supposed to indicate lead by its presence. Found in Atchison, Christian, Clark, Clinton, Greene, Henry, Holt, Howell, Jackson, Jasper, Lawrence, Madison, McDonald, Newton, Pike, Shannon, St. Louis, Webster and Wright counties.

**181. Amorpha fruticosa L.**

*False indigo.* A taller shrub than the last, found along rocky banks and branches throughout the State. It has been found in Atchison, Clark, Dunklin, Jackson, Jasper, Lawrence, Lewis, Madison, McDonald, New Madrid, Newton, Oregon, Pike, Shannon, St. Louis, Stoddard and Webster counties.

**182. Kraunhia frutescens (L.) Greene.**

*Wistaria.* A tall vigorous climber of the lowlands of the southeastern part of the State. Often seen in cultivaton, and is almost as handsome as the Chinese species. It is found in Butler, Dunklin and Mississippi counties. Also reported from Ray county by Broadhead, but that must have been a mistake. This is *Wistaria frutescens* Poir.

**183. Robinia Pseudacacia L.**

*Common locust.* A well-known, handsome tree, commonly cultivated, and escaped in many places in the State. It is found native in the southwestern part of the State—in Barry, Jasper, McDonald, Newton, Stone and Taney counties. It has been found growing spontaneously in Andrew, Atchison, Cape Girardeau, Carroll, Cass, Clark, Clay, Greene, Jackson, Miller, Ray and St. Louis counties.

## RUE FAMILY (RUTACEÆ).

**184. Xanthoxylum Americanum Mill.**

*Prickly ash.* A well-known shrub found in many places in the State, but appearing to be absent from the southwestern part. Has been found in Atchison,

Butler, Clark, Clay, Daviess, Dunklin, Holt, Jackson, Livingston, Madison, Miller, Pike, Ray, Scotland, Shannon, St. Charles, St. Louis and Wayne counties.

### 185. Ptelea trifoliata L.

*Hop tree—Wafer ash.* A shrub or small tree found in the State south and east of a line drawn from the northeast corner to the southwest. Is found in Atchison, Butler, Carter, Clark, Greene, McDonald, Miller, Pike, Shannon, St. Francois, St. Louis and Wayne counties.

### SIMARUBA FAMILY ( SIMARUBACEÆ ).

### 186. Ailanthus glandulosa Desf.

*Tree of Heaven.* Formerly much planted, and as it was found to spread by the root very badly, it has been discontinued. Reported as growing spontaneously in Cape Girardeau, Dunklin, Greene, Howell, Jackson, McDonald, St. Louis and Wayne counties.

### CASHEW FAMILY ( ANACARDIACEÆ ).

### 187. Cotinus cotinoides ( Nutt.) Britton.

*Smoke-tree.* A tall shrub or small tree, very much resembling the cultivated *Rhus cotinus*, which has been found in Mississippi county. Also reported from St. Louis county by Broadhead, but that must have been the real Smoke-tree in cultivation. This is *Rhus cotinoides* Nutt.

### 188. Rhus aromatica Ait.

*Sweet sumach.—Polecat bush.* A low species of Sumach found in rocky places in woods, and in the prairie regions. Is found in Clark, Greene, Howell, Jackson, Livingston, McDonald, Miller, Oregon, Pike, Scotland, Shannon, St. Francois, St. Louis, Wayne and Webster counties.

### 189. Rhus copallina L.

*Copal sumach.* A well-known species of Sumach in the prairie regions, where it often gets to be 20 feet in height, and much taller than *Rhus glabra*, commonly called Black sumach. Has been found in Atchison, Barry, Barton, Bollinger, Butler, Carter, Christian, Dade, Dunklin, Greene, Howell, Jackson, Jasper, Lawrence, Madison, McDonald, Miller, Mississippi, Newton, Oregon, Pike, Ray, Shannon, St. Francois, St. Louis, Stoddard, Texas, Wayne, Webster and Wright counties.

### 190. Rhus glabra L.

*Smooth sumach—White sumach.* Another well-known shrub, found throughout the State, in all kinds of soil. It is found in Andrew, Atchison, Barry, Barton, Bollinger, Buchanan, Butler, Cape Girardeau, Carroll, Christian, Clark, Clay, Dade, Dunklin, Greene, Holt, Howell, Jackson, Jasper, Jefferson, Lawrence, Livingston, Madison, McDonald, Miller, Mississippi, New Madrid, Newton, Oregon, Pike, Platte, Ray, Ripley, Scotland, Scott, Shannon, St. Charles, St. Francois, St. Louis, Stoddard, Texas, Washington, Wayne, Webster and Wright counties.

### 191. Rhus hirta ( L.) Sudw.

*Staghorn sumach.* Although credited to our region by Gray's Manual, I have never seen it. This is *Rhus typhina* L.

192.  Rhus radicans L.

*Poison ivy—Poison oak.* Too well-known to need any description, but as the Virginian Creeper is often mistaken for this, I will say that this species has only three leaflets, while the Virginian Creeper has five. Has been found in Adair, Atchison, Barry, Barton, Bollinger, Buchanan, Butler, Cape Girardeau, Chariton, Clark, Clay, Dade, Dunklin, Greene, Holt, Howell, Jackson, Jasper, Jefferson, Lawrence, Livingston, Madison, McDonald, Miller, Mississippi, New Madrid, Oregon, Pike, Platte, Ray, Scotland, Shannon, St. Francois, St. Louis, Stoddard, Texas, Wayne and Webster counties. This is *Rhus toxicodendron* L.

193.  Rhus Vernix L.

*Poison sumach—Poison elder.* A very poisonous species, which has been reported from Greene county, but probably erroneously. This is *Rhus venenata* D. C.

## HOLLY FAMILY (Aquifoliaceæ).

194.  Ilex decidua Walt.

*Wild privet.* A tall shrub or small tree, mostly confined to the lowlands of the southeastern part of the State. Has been found in Bollinger, Butler, Cape Girardeau, Dunklin, McDonald, Miller, Mississippi, New Madrid, Ripley, St. Louis, Stoddard and Wayne counties.

195.  Ilex lævigata (Pursh) A. Gray.

*Smooth winterberry.* Has been reported from Pike county, but I have not seen it in the state.

196.  Ilex opaca Ait.

*Holly.* A beautiful small evergreen tree of the lowlands of the southeastern part of the state. Often seen in cultivation, when it is an attractive tree. It is found in Butler, Cape Girardeau, Dunklin, Mississippi, New Madrid and Stoddard counties. Also, reported from Cooper county by Swallow, but these must have been trees that were planted there.

197.  Ilex verticillata (L.) A. Gray.

*Black Alder. Winterberry.* A small shrub which has been found in Boone, Iron, Mississippi and Pike counties.

## STAFF-TREE FAMILY (Celastraceæ).

198.  Euonymus Americanus L.

*Strawberry bush.* A small shrub found in the southeastern part of the state. The fruit resembles a strawberry when it bursts open, whence the common name. Has been found in Boone, Butler, Dunklin, Mississippi, New Madrid and St. Charles counties. Well worthy of a place among our ornamental plants, and sometimes found in cultivation.

199.  Euonymus atropurpureus Jacq.

*Burning bush. Waahoo.* A larger shrub than the last, and one more widely distributed over the State. It is common in cultivation already, and also is a desirable ornamental plant for shrubberies. It is found in Adair, Atchison, Butler, Clark, Clay, Daviess, Dunklin, Greene, Holt, Jackson, Jasper, Livingston, Madison, McDonald, Newton, Pike, Ray, Stoddard, Shannon, St. Louis and Wayne counties.

200.   Euonymus obovatus Nutt.

*Trailing strawberry bush.* A procumbent species which has been found in Dunklin and Shannon counties. This is *Euonymus Americanus obovatus* Torr. and Gray.

201.   Celastrus scandens L.

*Bitter-sweet.* A beautiful ornamental vine found in many places in the state, and bearing beautiful fruit. Very common in cultivation in shrubberies. Has been found in Adair, Atchison, Cass, Clark, Clay, Dunklin, Jackson, McDonald, Miller, Newton, Oregon, Pike and St. Louis counties.

## BLADDERWORT FAMILY (Staphyleaceæ).

202.   Staphylea trifolia L.

*Bladder nut.* A rather attractive and ornamental shrub, with a profusion of greenish-white flowers and a curious inflated pod. Is found in Adair, Andrew, Atchison, Butler, Cass, Clark, Dunklin, Jackson, Jasper, Madison, McDonald, Miller, Newton, Oregon, Pike, Ray, Shannon and St. Louis counties.

## MAPLE FAMILY (Aceraceæ).

203.   Acer Drummondii H. v A.

*Texas maple.* A Southern species lately ascertained to be very common to the lowlands of the southeastern part of the State. Has been found in Cape Girardeau, Dunklin, Mississippi, New Madrid, Scott and Stoddard counties.

204.   Acer Negundo L.

*Box-elder.* A fast-growing beautiful ornamental tree, found throughout the State along river bottoms and smaller streams. It reaches its greatest development in the lowlands of the southeastern part of the State, where there are trees three to four feet in diameter. It occurs in Adair, Andrew, Atchison, Bollinger, Buchanan, Butler, Cape Girardeau, Clay, Dade, Daviess, Dunklin, Holt, Jackson, Jasper, Jefferson, Livingston, McDonald, Miller, Newton, Oregon, Pike, Platte, Ray, Scotland, Shannon, St. Louis, Stoddard, Washington and Wayne counties. This is *Negundo aceroides* Moench.

205.   Acer nigrum Michx. f.

*Black sugar maple.* A large, valuable tree, found throughout the State and including almost all of our sugar maples. It is the characteristic sugar maple of the western part of the state, where it occurs in large groves, almost to the exclusion of the eastern species. It is found in Boone, Butler, Cape Girardeau, Clay, Jackson, Madison, Newton, St. Louis, Washington and Wayne counties. This is *Acer saccharinum nigrum* Torr. and Gray.

206.   Acer Pennsylvanicum L.

*Striped maple.* A small, slender tree, which has been reported from Iron county, but I have not seen it.

207.   Acer rubrum L.

*Red maple.* A nice ornamental tree, found in the State south and east of a line drawn from Louisiana to Joplin. Occurs in Bollinger, Butler, Callaway,

Dunklin, Howell, Madison, McDonald, Miller, Mississippi, New Madrid, Shannon, St. Francois, St. Louis, Stoddard, Wayre and Wright counties.

### 208.  Acer saccharinum L.

*Silver maple.*  A very fine ornamental tree, found in many places in the state along streams, and very common in cultivation  *Populus alba*, the Abele or White Popular is often erroneously called Silver Maple.  The Silver Maple occurs in Adair, Andrew, Atchison, Barton, Butler, Chariton, Clark, Clay, Daviess, Dunklin, Holt, Jackson, Jefferson, Livingston, Madison, McDona'd, Mississippi, New Madrid, Newter, Pike, Platte, Ray, Scotland, St. Francois, St. Louis, Stoddard and Washington counties.  This is *Acer dasycarpum* Ehrh.

### 209.  Acer saccharum L.

*Sugar maple.*  This is the real Sugar maple, as we are accustomed to see in the east, but which is rarely found so far west as our region.  Has been found in St. Louis ccurty.  This is *Acer saccharinum* Wang.

### 210.  Acer saccharum barbatum (Michx.) Trelease.

*Sugar maple.*  A fine, large, valuable tree, very common in cultivation and an universal favorite.  Michaux first recognized this distinct species, and lately it has been brought out again, after having been neglected for ninety years.  It is found in Adair, Andrew, Bollinger, Buchanan, Callaway, Cape Girardeau, Clark, Daviess, Dunklin, Jackson, Livingston, Madison, McDonald, Miller, Pike, Shannon, St. Charles, St. Francois, St. Louis and Wayne counties.

## HORSE–CHESTNUT FAMILY (HIPPOCASTANACEÆ).

### 211.  Æsculus arguta Buckley.

*Texas buckeye.*  A southern species which extends as far north and east as our region, and has been found in Cass and Jackson counties.  It may be recognized by its habit of flowering from four feet high up to a small tree.

### 212.  Æsculus glabra Willd.

*Ohio Buckeye.*  The common buckeye of the northern and eastern part of the State, and extending as far west as the mouth of the Kansas river, where it is uncommon.  It does not flower until much larger than the last.  It is found in Adair, Bollinger, Clark, Greene, Howard, Jackson, Miller and St. Louis counties.

### 213.  Æsculus octandra Marsh.

*Sweet buckeye.*  An eastern species, which has been found in St. Louis county, but I have not seen it.  This is *Æsculus flava* Ait.

### 214.  Æsculus Pavia L.

*Red buckeye.*  A small shrub bearing bright red flowers, and confined to the lowlands of the southeastern part of the state.  Has been found in Bollinger, Butler, Cape Girardeau, Carter, Dunklin, Madison, Ripley, Stoddard and Wayne counties.

## SOAP-BERRY FAMILY (SAPINDACEÆ).

### 215.  Sapindus marginatus Willd.

*Soap-berry.*  A tall, slender tree of the southwest, much resembling a sumach, which has been found in McDonald county.

## BUCKTHORN FAMILY (Rhamnaceæ).

**216.  Berchemia scandens ( Hill) Trelease.**

*Supple-jack.* A tall, twining, very tough and flexible shrub of the lowlands of the southeastern part of the state. Is found in Butler, Dunklin, New Madrid, Shannon and Stone counties. This is *Berchemia volubilis* D. C.

**217.  Rhamnus Caroliniana Walt.**

*Southern buckthorn.* Like the last, the range of this species is to the southeast, and it is found in Dunklin, Iron, Madison, St. Louis and Wright counties.

**218.  Rhamnus lanceolata Pursh.**

*Buckthorn.* A tall shrub, found mostly in the western part of the State, usually along rocky branches and bluffs. Occurs in Atchison, Boone, Clark, Greene, Jackson, Jefferson, Lafayette, McDonald, Shannon and Wayne counties.

**219.  Ceanothus Americanus L.**

*New Jersey tea.* A low shrub, found in dry ground in many places in the State. Has been found in Adair, Atchison, Clark, Greene, Howell, Jackson, Jasper, Livingston, McDonald, Newton, Oregon, Pike, shannon, St. Louis, Webster and Wright counties.

**220.  Ceanothus ovatus Desf.**

*Redroot.* A rather taller shrub than the last, and confined to the western part of the State. Is found in Atchison, Cass, Scott, Jackson, McDonald and Shannon counties.

**221.  Ceanothus ovatus pubescens Torr. and Gray.**

*Redroot.* A variety of the last, which has been found in Atchison and Holt counties.

## VINE FAMILY (Vitaceæ).

**222.  Vitis æstivalis Michx.**

*Summer grape.* A fine grape, the parent of many varieties in cultivation. It is found in Butler, Clark, Dunklin, Howard, Howell, Jackson, Jasper, Madison, McDonald, Miller, Newton, Oregon, Pike, Ray, Shannon, St. Francois, St. Louis, Webster and Wayne counties.

**223.  Vitis bicolor LeConte.**

*Summer grape.* A much finer and larger grape than the last, and one that I do not know of having been used in cultivation. It is mostly confined to the southwestern part of the State, and has been found in Carter and McDonald counties. This is *Vitis æstivalis bicolor* LeConte.

**224.  Vitis cinerea Engelm.**

*Downy grape.* A strong-growing grape-vine in the rich bottoms along the Missouri and Mississippi rivers, and also some of the smaller streams. Has been found in Cape Girardeau, Clay, Dunklin, Jackson, St. Francois and St. Louis counties.

**225. Vitis cordifolia Michx.**

*Frost grape, Winter grape* The largest of our grape-vines, and the widest distributed; occurs in many places in the State along river banks. It has been found in Atchison, Bollinger, Butler, Cape Girardeau, Dunklin, Howard, Howell, Iron, Jackson, Jasper, Lewis, Livingston, Madison, McDonald, Miller, Newton, Oregon, Pike, Ray, Shannon, St. Charles, St Francois and St. Louis counties.

**226. Vitis palmata Vahl.**

*Swamp grape.* A smaller vine than any of the others, and found only in the deep bottoms adjacent to the Mississippi river; occurs in Butler, Dunklin, Jefferson, New Madrid, St. Charles and St. Louis counties.

**227. Vitis rotundifolia Michx.**

*Muscadine.* A high-climbing slender grape-vine, which is confined to the lowlands of the southeastern part of the State. Is found in Dunklin and Madison counties. Has been reported from Marles and Montgomery counties by Broadhead, but that evidently was a mistake.

**228. Vitis rupestris Scheele.**

*Sand grape.* A mostly procumbent species found along gravelly or sandy branches in the southern part of the State. Occurs in Franklin, Howell, Jefferson, McDonald, Pike and Shannon counties.

**229. Vitis vulpina L.**

*Slough grape.* A common grape-vine in the western part of the State along the Missouri river, and other smaller streams. It is found in Andrew, Atchison, Howard, Pike, Platte, St. Charles and St. Louis counties. This is *Vitis riparia* Michx.

**230. Parthenocissus quinquefolia (L). Planch.**

*Virginian creeper* A handsome ornamental climber, often seen in cultivation, where it is quite attractive. It has been found in Atchison, Buchanan, Butler, Cape Girardeau, Clark, Clay, Dunklin, Greene, Howell, Jackson, Madison, McDonald, Miller, Mississippi, Newton, Oregon, Pike, Ray, Scotland, Shannon, St. Francois, St. Louis, Wayne and Webster counties. This is *Ampelopsis quinquefolia* Michx.

**231. Ampelopsis arborea (L.) Rusby.**

*Cissus.* A large, strong-growing vine, found in the State only in the southern part. Occurs in Butler, Cape Girardeau, Jefferson, New Madrid and Pemiscot counties. This is *Cissus stans* Pers.

**232. Ampelopsis cordata Michx.**

*Cissus.* A kind of false grape-vine, found mostly in the western part of the State along streams. Occurs in Clay, Cooper, Greene, Jackson, Jasper, McDonald, Miller, Newton, Oregon, Platte, Ray, Shannon and St. Louis counties. This is *Cissus Ampelopsis* Pers.

H—25

## LINDEN FAMILY (TILIACEÆ).

### 233.   Tilia Americana L.

*Linden.*  A fine, large, valuable tree, found in many places throughout the State, except, perhaps, the southwestern part, where it appears to be absent.  It is most common along the Missouri river on the bluffs.  Occurs in Adair, Andrew, Atchison, Bates, Butler, Daviess, Dunklin, Holt, Howard, Jackson, Madison, Miller, Pike, Ray, Scotland, Shannon, St. Charles, St. Francois. St. Louis, Sullivan and Wayne counties.

### 234.   Tilia heterophylla Vent.

*White basswood.*  Has been collected in the State by Swallow, but I have not seen it.

## ST. JOHN'S-WORT FAMILY (HYPERICACEÆ).

### 235.   Ascyrum hypericoides L.

*St. Andrew's Cross.*  A low shrub found only in the southern part of the State. Is found in Butler, Carter, Dunklin, Greene, McDonald, New Madrid, Sullivan and Wayne counties.  This is *Ascyrum Crux-Andreæ L.*

### 236.   Hypericum prolificum L.

*Shrubby St. John's-wort.*  A tall, shrubby species, which is only found in the southeastern part of the State.  Has been found in Butler, Carter, Clark, Howell, Iron, Madison, Randolph, Shannon, St. Louis, Washington and Wayne counties.

### 237.   Hypericum sphærocarpum Michx.

*St. John's-wort.*  A low species, found in many places in the State, usually in dry or rocky ground.  Is found in Barry, Barton, Boone, Butler, Cass, Clark, Greene, Jackson, Jasper, McDonald, Newton, Pike, Shannon, St. Louis, Washington and Wayne counties.

## MEZEREUM FAMILY (THYMELEACEÆ).

### 238.   Dirca palustris L.

*Leatherwood—Moosewood.*  A well-known curious shrub with brittle wood, and very tough fibrous bark, found only in the southern part of the State along rocky banks of streams.  Occurs in Barry, Callaway, Dunklin, Iron, Madison, Perry, Shannon, Stone, Taney, Warren and Wayne counties.

## GINSENG FAMILY (ARALIACEÆ)

### 239.   Aralia spinosa L.

*Angelica-tree—Tear blanket.*  A tall, slender, very prickly tree, confined to the low lands of the southeastern part of the State.  Has been found in Bollinger, Butler, Cape Girardeau, Dunklin, Madison, Mississippi, Ripley, Stoddard and Wayne counties.  Also reported from St. Louis county by Murtfeldt, but that evidently must have been in cultivation.

## DOGWOOD FAMILY (CORNACEÆ).

### 240. Cornus alternifolia L. f.

*Alternate-leaved dogwood.* A species of the northeastern states, but reaching our borders in Clark county.

### 241. Cornus Amomum Mill.

*Kinnikinnik.* A slender, red-stemmed species of dogwood found in swampy places, and usually called Swamp dogwood. It is found in Atchison, Buchanan, Clark, Clay, Greene, Jackson, McDonald, Newton, Oregon, Pike, Scotland, Shannon and Webster counties. This is *Cornus sericea L.*

### 242. Cornus asperifolia Michx.

*Rough-leaved dogwood.* A tall shrub found in abundance along the bottoms of the Missouri river, especially in the western part of the State. Occurs in Andrew, Atchison, Buchanan, Clark, Dunklin, Scott, Jackson, Jasper, Livingston, McDonald, Pike, Platte and Shannon counties.

### 243. Cornus candidissima Marsh.

*Panicled dogwood.* A slender dogwood, found along streams throughout the State. Has been found in Buchanan, Butler, Cape Girardeau, Clark, Clay, Dunklin, Jackson, Jefferson, McDonald, Miller, Oregon, Pike, Ray, Shannon, St. Louis and Stoddard counties. This is *Cornus paniculata L'Her.*

### 244. Cornus circinata L'Her.

*Round-leaved dogwood.* Has been reported from several places in the State, but I have not seen it.

### 245. Cornus florida L.

*Flowering dogwood.* A tall shrub or small tree, very well known, and found principally in the southern part of the State. Does not appear to grow in the northern or western part, and its range may be said to be fairly that of the Sassafras. It is found in Bollinger, Boone, Butler, Callaway, Cape Girardeau, Carter, Cedar, Cole, Dunklin, Greene, Howard, Howell, Jasper, Madison, McDonald, Miller, Mississippi, Montgomery, New Madrid, Newton, Oregon, Pemiscot, Pettis, Pike, Saline, Scott, Shannon, St. Francois, St. Louis, Stoddard, Texas, Wayne, Webster and Wright counties.

### 246. Cornus stricta Lam.

*Stiff dogwood.* A lowland species confined to the lowlands of the southeastern part of the State. Has been found in Cape Girardeau, Dunklin, New Madrid and Stoddard counties.

### 247. Nyssa aquatica L.

*Black gum.* A valuable tree found in the southeastern part of the State. It is found in Benton, Bollinger, Butler, Cape Girardeau, Carter, Dunklin, Howell, Madison, Maries, McDonald, Mississippi, New Madrid, Newton, Oregon, Perry, Shannon, St. Francois, Stoddard, Wayne and Wright counties. This is *Nyssa sylvatica Marsh.*

248.   Nyssa uniflora Wang.

*Tupelo.*  A tall slender tree found in the swamps of the southeastern part of the State.  Not of any value for lumber, as it never reaches any size for cutting.  It grows in Butler, Cape Girardeau, Dunklin, Mississippi, New Madrid, Shannon and Stoddard counties.

## HEATH FAMILY ( ERICACEÆ ).

249.   Azalea nudiflora L.

*Purple azalea.*  A very pretty azalea, which has only been found in Madison county.  This is *Rhododendron nudiflorum* Torr.

250.   Leucothœ racemosa ( L. ) A. Gray.

*Leucothœ.*  A tall shrub, which has also been found in Madison county.

251.   Arctostaphylos Uva-ursi ( L. ) Spreng.

*Bearberry.*  A smooth trailing shrub, which has been reported from the State, but I have not seen it.

252.   Gaylussacia dumosa ( Andr. ) Torr. & Gray.

*Dwarf huckleberry.*  Has been reported from Newton county, but this also I have not seen.

253.   Gaylussacia resinosa ( Ait. ) Torr. & Gray.

*Black huckleberry.*  Has been reported from Miller county and other places in the State, but this too I have not seen.

254.   Vaccinium arboreum Marsh.

*Farkleberry.*  A small tree in this State, bearing berries that ripen toward winter, hence called Winter huckleberries.  It is found in Butler, Carter, Dunklin, Howell, Iron, McDonald, Newton, Perry, Stoddard and Wayne counties.

255.   Vaccinium corymbosum L.

*Common blueberry.*  A tall shrub, which has been found in Greene, Iron and Shannon counties.

256.   Vaccinium Pennsylvanicum Lam.

*Dwarf blueberry.*  A low species, which has been found in Shannon county, and several other places in the State.

257.   Vaccinium stamineum L.

*Deerberry—Buckberry.*  A low shrub found only in the Ozark region.  Occurs in Carter, Howell, Iron, McDonald, Newton, Pike, Shannon and St. Francois counties.

258.   Vaccinium vacillans Kalm.

*Huckleberry.*  This is the species which produces the abundant crops of berries in this State which are called Huckleberries.  It only occurs in the Ozark region, and is found in Bollinger, Boone, Callaway, Carter, Cole, Henry, Howard, Howell, Iron, Jasper, Lincoln, McDonald, Morgan, Oregon, Pike, Shannon, St. Charles, St. Louis and Webster counties.

259.   Vaccinium virgatum tenellum (Ait.) A. Gray.

*Blueberry.*  A low species which has been found in Shannon county.

## SAPODILLA FAMILY (Sapotaceæ).

260. Bumelia lanuginosa (Michx.) Pers.

*Buckthorn.* A spiny tree, 40 or 50 feet in height, found in the State south of a line drawn from Louisiana to Nevada. Occurs in Barton, Cedar, Cole, Franklin, Greene, Jasper, Jefferson, Madison, McDonald, Oregon, Shannon, St. Charles, St. Lou's, Warren and Wright counties.

261. Bumelia lycioides (L.) Pers.

*Southern buckthorn.* A southern species, which has been reported from the southeastern part of the State. *Bumelia tenax* Willd., reported from Miller county, is probably the last species.

## EBONY FAMILY (Ebenaceæ).

262. Diospyros Virginiana L.

*Persimmon.* A well-known tree with luscious fruit, which is quite promising for cultivation. The fruit is very variable in size, quality and earliness of ripening. In Dunklin county, where I observed it very closely one year, there was some very fine fruit that was ripe and gone before frost, and other equally as fine that did not ripen until it frosted. Others again were indifferent and did not ripen until they were frozen. It is found throughout the state, except perhaps in the northwestern part where it appears to be absent. It is found in Barry, Barton, Bollinger, Butler, Cape Girardeau, Carroll, Carter, Clay, Dade, Dunklin, Greene, Howell, Jackson, Jasper, Jefferson, Linn, Madison, McDonald, Miller, Mississippi, New Madrid, Newton, Pike, Ray, Shannon, St. Francois, St. Louis, Stoddard, Wayne and Wright counties.

## STORAX FAMILY (Styraceæ).

263. Styrax Americana Lam.

*Storax.* A small southern shrub, lately found in Butler, Dunklin and New Madrid counties.

## OLIVE FAMILY (Oleaceæ).

264. Fraxinus Americana L.

*White ash.* A large and valuable tree, found throughout the State in various kinds of soils. Reaches its greatest development in the lowlands of the southeastern part of the state, where there are trees three feet in diameter and 100 feet in height. It has been found in Atchison, Butler, Clark, Dunklin, Greene, Holt, Jackson, Lafayette, Livingston, Madison, McDonald, Miller, Mississippi, Newton, Oregon, Pike, Ripley, Shannon, St. Francois, St. Louis and Webster counties.

265. Fraxinus Americana profunda B. F. Bush.

*Swamp ash.* A species of ash which grows in the swamps of the southeastern part of the State, almost to the exclusion of the other species. In habit it is much like the Tupelo, having swelled butts and thick branchlets. It has been found in Dunklin, New Madrid and Stoddard counties.

266.   Fraxinus lanceolata Borck.

*Green ash.* A large, valuable ash, found throughout the State in bottoms along streams. Reaches its greatest development along the overflowed bottoms of the Missouri river in the western part of the State, where there are trees 150 feet in height and five feet in diameter. It occurs in Atchison, Bollinger, Boone, Butler, Clark, Dunklin, Holt, Jackson, McDonald, Mississippi, Newton, Platte, Ralls, Scotland, Shannon, St. Francois and Wayne counties. Hitchcock described a variety *pubescens* from St. Louis county, and I had adopted the name for the downy-leaved form of our tree; but, unfortunately, his description and observations were based on depauperate specimens of the Blue ash, which, according to Eggert, bore one year fertile flowers, and sterile the next. This is *Fraxinus viridis* Michx. f.

267.   Fraxinus nigra Marsh.

*Black ash.* A small-sized tree with very tough wood, which has been found in Boone, Butler, Callaway, Cedar and Greene counties. This is *Fraxinus sambucifolia* Lam.

268.   Fraxinus Pennsylvanica Marsh.

*Red ash.* A small-sized ash, which has been found in Atchison, Jackson, Saline and St. Louis counties. This is *Fraxinus pubescens* Lam.

269.   Fraxinus quadrangulata Michx. f.

*Blue ash.* A small tree found in the State, mostly in the eastern and southern parts, and apparently absent from the western and northwestern. Has been found in Butler, Chariton, Greene, Howard, Iron, Jefferson, McDonald, Mississippi, Pike, Ralls, Randolph, Shannon, St. Louis and Washington counties.

270.   Adelia acuminata Michx.

*Adelia.* A small, spiny tree, found mostly in the southeastern part of the State. Occurs in Butler, Dunklin, Jefferson, New Madrid, Pike and St. Louis counties. This is *Forestiera acuminata* Poir.

271.   Chionanthus Virginica L.

*Fringe-tree.* A beautiful tree in cultivation, and which has been found in Mississippi county. `

## DOGBANE FAMILY (APOCYNACEÆ).

272.   Trachelospermum difforme (Walt.) A. Gray.

*Trachelospermum.* A high, twining plant of the Southern states, which has lately been found in Dunklin county.

## NIGHTSHADE FAMILY (SOLANACEÆ).

273.   Lycium vulgare (Ait. f.) Dunal.

*Matrimony-vine.* Commonly cultivated in gardens, and has escaped into waste places in Buchanan, Greene, Jackson and St. Louis counties.

## BIGNONIA FAMILY (BIGNONIACEÆ).

274.   Bignonia crucigera L.

*Cross-vine.* A tall, straight, climbing vine of the Southern states, which is found in the lowlands of the southeastern part of the State. Occurs in Bollinger, Butler, Cape Girardeau, Iron and St. Louis counties. This is *Bignonia capreolata* L.

TREES, SHRUBS AND VINES OF MISSOURI. 391

**275. Tecoma radicans (L.) D. C.**

*Trumpet Creeper.* A beautiful vine, found in the southern part of the State, mostly along streams. It is found in Bates, Bollinger, Cape Girardeau, Christian, Dade, Dunklin, Greene, Howard, Jackson, Jasper, Jefferson, Johnson, Madison, Marion, McDonald, Miller, Mississippi, New Madrid, Newton, Oregon, Pike, Scott, Shannon, St. Charles, St. Francois, St. Louis, Stoddard and Wayne counties.

**276. Catalpa Catalpa (L.) Karst.**

*Catalpa.* A species much planted for ornament, and which has escaped in Jackson and St. Louis counties. This is *Catalpa bignonioides* Walt.

**277. Catalpa speciosa Warder.**

*Hardy catalpa.* A large valuable tree of the lowlands of the southeastern part of the State, where it is found in Bollinger, Cape Girardeau, Dunklin, Madison, Mississippi, New Madrid, Scott and Stoddard counties.

## MADDER FAMILY (RUBIACEÆ).

**278. Cephalanthus occidentalis L.**

*Button bush.* A small shrub, or in the swamps of the southeastern part of the State a small tree, found all over the State in wet places and along streams. It has been found in Adair, Andrew, Atchison, Barton, Bollinger, Buchanan, Cape Girardeau, Carter, Cass, Chariton, Clark, Dade, Dunklin, Holt, Jackson, Jasper, Lawrence, Livingston, Macon, McDonald, Mississippi, New Madrid, Newton, Oregon, Pike, Scotland, Scott, Shannon, St. Francois, St. Louis, Stoddard and Wayne counties.

**279. Mitchella repens L.**

*Partridge-berry.* A smooth creeping ever green shrub, which is found along the sandy banks of the swamps in the southeastern part of the State. It is found in Butler, Dunklin and New Madrid counties.

## HONEYSUCKLE FAMILY (CAPRIFOLIACEÆ).

**280. Sambucus Canadensis L.**

*Common elder.* A well-known shrub, which is found all over the State. Is found in Andrew, Atchison, Barry, Bollinger, Buchanan, Butler, Cape Girardeau, Carroll, Clark, Clay, Dunklin, Greene, Holt, Jackson, Jefferson, Lawrence, Livingston, Madison, McDonald, Miller, Mississippi, New Madrid, Newton, Oregon, Pike, Platte, Ray, Scott, Shannon, St. Charles, St. Francois, St. Louis, Stoddard and Wayne counties.

**281. Viburnum alnifolium Marsh.**

*Hobble-bush.* A straggling shrub, which has been found in Marion and St Louis counties. *Viburnum opulus* L., which was reported from St. Louis county by Murtfeldt, may have been this species. This is *Viburnum lantanoides* Michx.

**282. Viburnum dentatum L.**

*Arrow-wood.* A tall smooth shrub, which has been found in many places in the State. It occurs in Adair, Andrew, Grundy, Harrison, Knox, Lincoln, Marion, Monroe, Montgomery, Pike, Ralls, Shannon, Shelby and Worth counties.

### 283.  Viburnum Lentago L.

*Sheep-berry.* A well-known shrub or small tree, found in many places in the State, except perhaps the southeastern, where it is replaced by the next. It has been found in Adair, Cape Girardeau, Cass, Clark, Greene, Howell, Jackson, Jasper, Madison, McDonald, Miller, Newton, Ray, Scotland, Shannon and St. Louis counties.

### 284.  Viburnum prunifolium L.

*Black haw.* Also a well-known tree, but not distinguished from the last species by the country people, who call both Black haws. The range of this species is chiefly in the southern part of the State, and it abounds in the Ozark region, where the last is but rarely found. It has been found in Butler, Carter, Cass, Clark, DeKalb, Dunklin, Greene, Jackson, Jasper, McDonald, Miller, Newton, Oregon, Pike, Shannon, St. Louis, Stoddard, Wayne, Webster, Worth and Wright counties.

### 285.  Viburnum pubescens (Ait.) Pursh.

*Downy arrow-wood.* A small slender shrub, found on rocky banks along streams. It has been found only in Clark and Shannon counties.

### 286.  Symphoricarpus occidentalis Hook.

*Wolfberry.* A shrub similar to the Coral-berry, but bearing large white berries. Has been found in Atchison county.

### 287.  Symphoricarpus symphoricarpus (L.) MacM.

*Coral-berry. Indian currant.* A small bushy shrub with hard, tough roots, found all over the State, and commonly called Buck-bush by the country people. It is found in Adair, Atchison, Barry, Barton, Bollinger, Butler, Cape Girardeau, Carroll, Carter, Clark, Clay, Dade, Greene, Holt, Howell, Jackson, Jasper, Jefferson, Knox, Lawrence, Livingston, Madison, McDonald, Miller, Mississippi, New Madrid, Newton, Oregon, Pike, Platte, Ray, Scott, Shannon, St. Charles, St. Francois, St. Louis, Stoddard, Wayne, Webster and Wright counties. This is *Symphoricarpus vulgaris* Michx.

### 288.  Lonicera Caprifolium L.

*American Woodbine.* A very pretty Honeysuckle, which is often found in the Ozark region. Occurs in Carter, Daviess, McDonald and Shannon counties. This is *Lonicera grata Ait.*

### 289.  Lonicera dioica L.

*Small Honeysuckle.* Another very pretty Honeysuckle, which has been found in Buchanan, Clark, Jackson, Pike, Ralls, Shannon and St. Louis counties. This is *Lonicera glauca Hill.*

### 290.  Lonicera hirsuta Eaton.

*Hairy Honeysuckle.* Has been found in Ralls county.

### 291.  Lonicera hirsuta Eaton.  .

*Japanese Honeysuckle.* Commonly cultivated, and has run wild in Butler and Mississippi counties.

**292. Lonicera sempervirens L.**

*Trumpet Honeysuckle.* Commonly cultivated, and has escaped into copses in Jackson county.

**293. Lonicera Sullivantii A. Gray.**

*Sullivant's Honeysuckle.* Has been reported from Cass county.

## GRASS FAMILY (GRAMINEÆ).

**294. Arundinaria tecta (Walt.) Muhl.**

*Small Cane—Switch Cane* A well-known woody grass, very common in the Southeastern part of the state, and not infrequent in the Southern and Southwestern. This family should properly have headed this list, but was overlooked, and so I insert it here. The Big Cane, *Arundinaria macrosperma* has been reported as occurring in the state by Swallow, but there is no evidence to show that it does grow in the state, although it cannot be very far from our Southeastern limits.

A number of other woody plants have been reported and credited to the state, but there is not sufficient evidence to warrant me in including them in the list. It may be when we come to publish a second report on our woody plants that some of these doubtful things may be proved to actually occur within our limits.

# INDEX TO "TREES, SHRUBS AND VINES."

[The numbers refer to the numbers of the species.]

# V

INDEX.